Shakespeare in Three Steps
A Midsummer Night's Dream

by Sonya Shafer

Recommended for Grades 2–12
Comedy

Summary: This is the story of two young couples crossed in love, a kingdom of fairies, and a bumbling troupe of would-be actors who all have definite plans for one evening in summer. When the king of fairies and his favorite sprite decide to play a trick on his queen, chaos ensues for all and they must scramble to put everything to rights again.

Shakespeare in Three Steps: A Midsummer Night's Dream
© 2015 by Sonya Shafer

All rights reserved. However, we grant permission to make printed copies or use this work on multiple electronic devices for members of your immediate household. Quantity discounts are available for classroom and co-op use. Please contact us for details.

Cover Design: John Shafer and Sarah Shafer

ISBN 978-1-61634-279-1 printed
ISBN 978-1-61634-280-7 electronic download

Published by
Simply Charlotte Mason, LLC
930 New Hope Road #11-892
Lawrenceville, Georgia 30045
simplycharlottemason.com

Printed by PrintLogic, Inc.
Monroe, Georgia, USA

Contents

Shakespeare in Three Steps 5
Step 1: Read the story. 7
Step 2: Hear the script. 12
   Act I, Scene 1. 13
   Act I, Scene 2. 16
   Act II, Scene 1 18
   Act II, Scene 2. 21
   Act III, Scene 1 23
   Act III, Scene 2. 25
   Act IV, Scene 1 27
   Act IV, Scene 2 29
   Act V. 31
Step 3: Watch the play. 34
A Midsummer Night's Dream script 35

Shakespeare in Three Steps

Understand and enjoy Shakespeare's plays by following these three steps.

Step 1: Read the story.
   Read aloud the story version of the play to get familiar with the main characters and plot.

Step 2: Hear the script.
   Listen to each scene on the audio dramatization and follow along in the script, or assign students to read aloud the various characters' lines themselves.

Step 3: Watch the play.
   Enjoy a live or recorded presentation of the play.

Step 1: Read the story.

Ask students where on the calendar they might expect a festival called Midsummer to fall. Explain that Midsummer is celebrated around the summer solstice in June, the longest day of the year. This Shakespeare play is a mixture of fairies, magic, actors, and couples—a silly imaginative story that reminds us of something that someone might dream on Midsummer's night.

Read aloud the story version of *A Midsummer Night's Dream* below to get familiar with the main characters and plot. Feel free to divide the story in half, reading half now and the rest later. If desired, help the students create a list of the main characters with a brief description of who each one is to help them keep everybody straight in their minds as you go along.

A Midsummer Night's Dream
(from *Beautiful Stories from Shakespeare for Children* by E. Nesbit)

Hermia and Lysander were lovers; but Hermia's father wished her to marry another man, named Demetrius.

Now, in Athens, where they lived, there was a wicked law, by which any girl who refused to marry according to her father's wishes, might be put to death. Hermia's father was so angry with her for refusing to do as he wished, that he actually brought her before the Duke of Athens to ask that she might be killed, if she still refused to obey him. The Duke gave her four days to think about it, and, at the end of that time, if she still refused to marry Demetrius, she would have to die.

Lysander of course was nearly mad with grief, and the best thing to do seemed to him for Hermia to run away to his aunt's house at a place beyond the reach of that cruel law; and there he would come to her and marry her. But before she started, she told her friend, Helena, what she was going to do.

Helena had been Demetrius' sweetheart long before his marriage with Hermia had been thought of, and being very silly, like all jealous people, she could not see that it was not poor Hermia's fault that Demetrius wished to marry her instead of his own lady, Helena. She knew that if she told Demetrius that Hermia was going, as she was, to the wood outside Athens, he would follow her, "and I can follow him, and at least I shall see him," she said to herself. So she went to him, and betrayed her friend's secret.

Now this wood where Lysander was to meet Hermia, and where the other two had decided to follow them, was full of fairies, as most woods are, if one only had the eyes to see them, and in this wood on this night were the King and Queen of the fairies, Oberon and Titania. Now fairies are very wise people, but now and then they can be quite as foolish as mortal folk. Oberon and Titania, who might have been as happy as the days were long, had thrown away all their joy in a foolish quarrel. They never met

Notes

An alternate idea for younger children would be to read the picture book, A Midsummer Night's Dream, *retold by Bruce Coville, or listen to Jim Weiss' retelling on his audio recording,* Shakespeare for Children, *from Greathall Productions.*

simplycharlottemason.com

Notes

without saying disagreeable things to each other, and scolded each other so dreadfully that all their little fairy followers, for fear, would creep into acorn cups and hide them there.

So, instead of keeping one happy Court and dancing all night through in the moonlight, as is fairies' use, the King with his attendants wandered through one part of the wood, while the Queen with hers kept state in another. And the cause of all this trouble was a little Indian boy whom Titania had taken to be one of her followers. Oberon wanted the child to follow him and be one of his fairy knights; but the Queen would not give him up.

On this night, in a mossy moonlit glade, the King and Queen of the fairies met.

"Ill met by moonlight, proud Titania," said the King.

"What! jealous, Oberon?" answered the Queen. "You spoil everything with your quarreling. Come, fairies, let us leave him. I am not friends with him now."

"It rests with you to make up the quarrel," said the King. "Give me that little Indian boy, and I will again be your humble servant and suitor."

"Set your mind at rest," said the Queen. "Your whole fairy kingdom buys not that boy from me. Come, fairies."

And she and her train rode off down the moonbeams.

"Well, go your ways," said Oberon. "But I'll be even with you before you leave this wood."

Then Oberon called his favorite fairy, Puck. Puck was the spirit of mischief. He used to slip into the dairies and take the cream away, and get into the churn so that the butter would not come, and turn the beer sour, and lead people out of their way on dark nights and then laugh at them, and tumble people's stools from under them when they were going to sit down, and upset their hot ale over their chins when they were going to drink.

"Now," said Oberon to this little sprite, "fetch me the flower called Love-in-idleness. The juice of that little purple flower laid on the eyes of those who sleep will make them, when they wake, to love the first thing they see. I will put some of the juice of that flower on my Titania's eyes, and when she wakes she will love the first thing she sees, were it lion, bear, or wolf, or bull, or meddling monkey, or a busy ape."

While Puck was gone, Demetrius passed through the glade followed by poor Helena, and still she told him how she loved him and reminded him of all his promises, and still he told her that he did not and could not love her, and that his promises were nothing. Oberon was sorry for poor Helena, and when Puck returned with the flower, he bade him follow Demetrius and put some of the juice on his eyes, so that he might love Helena when he woke and looked on her, as much as she loved him. So Puck set off, and wandering through the wood found, not Demetrius, but Lysander, on whose eyes he put the juice; but when Lysander woke, he saw not his own Hermia, but Helena, who was walking through the wood looking for the cruel Demetrius; and directly he saw her he loved her and left his own lady, under the spell of the purple flower.

When Hermia woke she found Lysander gone, and wandered about the wood trying to find him. Puck went back and told Oberon what he had done, and Oberon soon found that he had made a mistake, and set about looking for Demetrius, and having found him, put some of the juice on his eyes. And the first thing Demetrius saw when he woke was also Helena. So now Demetrius and Lysander were both following her through the wood, and it was Hermia's turn to follow her lover as Helena had done before. The end of it was that Helena and Hermia began to quarrel, and Demetrius and Lysander went off to fight. Oberon was very sorry to see his kind scheme to help these lovers turn out so badly. So he said to Puck—

"These two young men are going to fight. You must overhang the night with drooping fog, and lead them so astray, that one will never find the other. When they are tired out, they will fall asleep. Then drop this other herb on Lysander's eyes. That will give him his old sight and his old love. Then each man will have the lady who loves him, and they will all think that this has been only a Midsummer Night's Dream. Then when this is done, all will be well with them."

So Puck went and did as he was told, and when the two had fallen asleep without meeting each other, Puck poured the juice on Lysander's eyes, and said:—

"When thou wakest,
Thou takest
True delight
In the sight
Of thy former lady's eye:
Jack shall have Jill;
Nought shall go ill."

Meanwhile Oberon found Titania asleep on a bank where grew wild thyme, oxlips, and violets, and woodbine, musk-roses and eglantine. There Titania always slept a part of the night, wrapped in the enameled skin of a snake. Oberon stooped over her and laid the juice on her eyes, saying:—

"What thou seest when thou wake,
Do it for thy true love take."

Now, it happened that when Titania woke the first thing she saw was a stupid clown, one of a party of players who had come out into the wood to rehearse their play. This clown had met with Puck, who had clapped an ass's head on his shoulders so that it looked as if it grew there. Directly Titania woke and saw this dreadful monster, she said, "What angel is this? Are you as wise as you are beautiful?"

"If I am wise enough to find my way out of this wood, that's enough for me," said the foolish clown.

"Do not desire to go out of the wood," said Titania. The spell of the love-juice was on her, and to her the clown seemed the most beautiful and delightful creature on all the earth. "I love you," she went on. "Come with me, and I will give you fairies to attend on you."

Notes

Notes

So she called four fairies, whose names were Peaseblossom, Cobweb, Moth, and Mustardseed.

"You must attend this gentleman," said the Queen. "Feed him with apricots and dewberries, purple grapes, green figs, and mulberries. Steal honey-bags for him from the humble-bees, and with the wings of painted butterflies fan the moonbeams from his sleeping eyes."

"I will," said one of the fairies, and all the others said, "I will."

"Now, sit down with me," said the Queen to the clown, "and let me stroke your dear cheeks, and stick musk-roses in your smooth, sleek head, and kiss your fair large ears, my gentle joy."

"Where's Peaseblossom?" asked the clown with the ass's head. He did not care much about the Queen's affection, but he was very proud of having fairies to wait on him. "Ready," said Peaseblossom.

"Scratch my head, Peaseblossom," said the clown. "Where's Cobweb?" "Ready," said Cobweb.

"Kill me," said the clown, "the red humble-bee on the top of the thistle yonder, and bring me the honey-bag. Where's Mustardseed?"

"Ready," said Mustardseed.

"Oh, I want nothing," said the clown. "Only just help Cobweb to scratch. I must go to the barber's, for methinks I am marvelous hairy about the face."

"Would you like anything to eat?" said the fairy Queen.

"I should like some good dry oats," said the clown—for his donkey's head made him desire donkey's food—"and some hay to follow."

"Shall some of my fairies fetch you new nuts from the squirrel's house?" asked the Queen.

"I'd rather have a handful or two of good dried peas," said the clown. "But please don't let any of your people disturb me; I am going to sleep."

Then said the Queen, "And I will wind thee in my arms."

And so when Oberon came along he found his beautiful Queen lavishing kisses and endearments on a clown with a donkey's head.

And before he released her from the enchantment, he persuaded her to give him the little Indian boy he so much desired to have. Then he took pity on her, and threw some juice of the disenchanting flower on her pretty eyes; and then in a moment she saw plainly the donkey-headed clown she had been loving, and knew how foolish she had been.

Oberon took off the ass's head from the clown, and left him to finish his sleep with his own silly head lying on the thyme and violets.

Thus all was made plain and straight again. Oberon and Titania loved each other more than ever. Demetrius thought of no one but Helena, and Helena had never had any thought of anyone but Demetrius.

As for Hermia and Lysander, they were as loving a couple as you could meet in a day's march, even through a fairy wood.

    So the four mortal lovers went back to Athens and were married; and the fairy King and Queen live happily together in that very wood at this very day.

Notes

Notes

We recommend The Arkangel Shakespeare audio dramatizations.

Step 2: Hear the script.

Make a copy of the script on pages 35–110 for each student who can read. Work your way through the script over several sittings, as outlined on the following pages. Each session will follow a sequence similar to the one below:

- Use the notes to introduce each scene. Highlight the featured lines if desired.

- Listen to the scene(s) on the audio dramatization and follow along in the script, or assign students to read aloud the various characters' lines themselves.

- Invite any questions or comments, then set it aside until next time.

Act I, Scene 1

❏ Ask students what they recall from last time's reading of the story of *A Midsummer Night's Dream*. Explain that the play divides the story into five parts, called Acts. Some of the acts are divided into smaller portions, called Scenes. Today they will listen to Act I, Scene 1. Read the scene summary to give students the context for the lines they will be hearing.

> *Scene Summary:* The play begins in the palace of the Duke, Theseus, who is looking forward to marrying his love, Hippolyta, in just four days. As you can imagine, it is hard for him to wait. He sends his servant to round up some entertainment for the festivities.
>
> Into his court enter Hermia, her father, Egeus, and two young men, Lysander and Demetrius. Egeus has brought them all to explain their predicament to the Duke and to ask him to talk some sense into Hermia. Egeus wants her to marry Demetrius, but she wishes to marry Lysander. According to the law there in Athens, Hermia must marry as her father has decreed; if she does not, she may be executed or sent to live in seclusion as a nun the rest of her life. Theseus gives her four days to make her decision.
>
> Lysander and Hermia secretly determine to make their way through the woods to Lysander's aunt's house and marry there, outside the boundaries of Athens and its laws. They confide their plans to Hermia's friend, Helena, who happens to be Demetrius' former sweetheart. Helena decides to inform Demetrius of their escape, hoping he will be grateful for the tip and grow to love her again.

❏ Distribute a copy of the script to each student who can read.

❏ (Optional) Take a sneak peek at these lines from the script and enjoy Shakespeare's wording.

  » Lines 93–94: Lysander knows that Egeus prefers Demetrius for a son-in-law, so he wryly makes this suggestion to his rival:

    You have her father's love, Demetrius;
    Let me have Hermia's: do you marry him.

  » Line 134: Upon having their hopes dashed, Lysander declares to Hermia that such is usually the case:

    The course of true love never did run smooth.

Notes

Shakespeare wrote the lines of his plays in both prose (conversational speaking) and poetry.

PERSON: *Prose lines will look like this.*

PERSON
Poetry lines will look like this.

Notes

» Lines 192–201 highlight the contrast between Hermia, Demetrius, and Helena as Hermia tries to discourage Demetrius from loving her and Helena tries to win his love.

HELENA
O, teach me how you look, and with what art
You sway the motion of Demetrius' heart.

HERMIA
I frown upon him, yet he loves me still.

HELENA
O that your frowns would teach my smiles such skill!

HERMIA
I give him curses, yet he gives me love.

HELENA
O that my prayers could such affection move!

HERMIA
The more I hate, the more he follows me.

HELENA
The more I love, the more he hateth me.

HERMIA
His folly, Helena, is no fault of mine.

HELENA
None, but your beauty: would that fault were mine!

» Lines 232–239 summarize what this play will demonstrate, that "Love looks not with the eyes, but with the mind."

Things base and vile, folding no quantity,
Love can transpose to form and dignity:
Love looks not with the eyes, but with the mind;
And therefore is wing'd Cupid painted blind:
Nor hath Love's mind of any judgement taste;
Wings and no eyes figure unheedy haste:
And therefore is Love said to be a child,
Because in choice he is so oft beguiled.

❑ Listen to Act I, Scene 1, on the audio dramatization (approx. 15 minutes) and follow along in the script, or assign students to read aloud the various characters' lines themselves. If you are assigning students to read aloud, the following list might be helpful; it details the characters who speak and the approximate number of lines each one has in this scene.

- Theseus, the Duke (64 lines)
- Hippolyta, the Duke's fiancé (5 lines)
- Egeus, the father (30 lines)
- Hermia, Egeus' daughter (56 lines)
- Lysander, Hermia's true love (53 lines)
- Demetrius, young man who wants to marry Hermia (2 lines)
- Helena, young woman who loves Demetrius (43 lines)

Notes

Notes

Act I, Scene 2

❏ Ask students what they recall from last time's reading about Hermia and Lysander's predicament and plans to wed. Explain that today they will listen to Act I, Scene 2. Read the scene summary to give students the context for the lines they will be hearing.

Scene Summary: Hermia and Lysander will not be the only ones in the woods that night. A troupe of actors has gathered in town, preparing a play to be performed at the Duke's wedding. In this scene, the lead actor is assigning parts to the other actors. They agree to meet in the woods later to rehearse.

❏ Distribute a copy of the script to each student who can read.

❏ (Optional) Take a sneak peek at these lines from the script and enjoy Shakespeare's wording.

» Line 15: When Nick Bottom wants the other actors to stop crowding around Quince, he tells them, "Masters, spread yourselves."

» Lines 21–23: Nick describes how his portrayal of the lover, Pyramus, will move the audience to tears.
That will ask some tears in the true performing of it:
if I do it, let the audience look to their eyes; I will move
storms, I will condole in some measure.

» Lines 38–44: Flute is hoping to avoid playing the part of a woman. In Shakespeare's day, only men acted in the plays, so some of them had to take the parts of women.

QUINCE: Flute, you must take Thisby on you.

FLUTE: What is Thisby? a wandering knight?

QUINCE: It is the lady that Pyramus must love.

FLUTE: Nay, faith, let me not play a woman; I have a
beard coming.

QUINCE: That's all one: you shall play it in a mask,
and you may speak as small as you will.

❑ Listen to Act I, Scene 2, on the audio dramatization (approx. 6 minutes) and follow along in the script, or assign students to read aloud the various characters' lines themselves. If you are assigning students to read aloud, the following list might be helpful; it details the characters who speak and the approximate number of lines each one has in this scene.

- Quince, director of the troupe (43 lines)
- Bottom, a vain and somewhat dimwitted actor (49 lines)
- Flute, actor (5 lines)
- Snug, actor (3 lines)
- Snout, actor (2 lines)
- Starveling, actor (2 lines)

Notes

Notes

Act II, Scene 1

❑ Ask students what they recall from last time's reading about the troupe of actors who are preparing a play for the Duke's wedding. Explain that at this point *A Midsummer Night's Dream* begins a new act as the focus shifts to the woods. Today they will listen to Act II, Scene 1. Read the scene summary to give students the context for the lines they will be hearing.

> *Scene Summary:* In the woods to which the lovers and the actors are headed, lives a kingdom of fairies. Their king and queen, however, are in the midst of a quarrel. Oberon, the fairy king, wants a little Indian boy whom the fairy queen, Titania, is raising as her own page. She will not give him over, and so Oberon and Titania, with their respective fairy followers, are not on good terms.
> Oberon sends a mischievous fairy named Puck to find a magical flower whose juice he will drop into Titania's eyes while she sleeps. Its effect will be that she will fall madly in love with the first living thing she sees when she wakes up. His plan is to withhold the antidote herb until she agrees to give him the little page-boy.
> While Puck is gone, Oberon overhears Helena pleading with Demetrius to love her and forget Hermia. He feels sorry for Helena and her unrequited love; so when Puck returns, the king takes some of the flower's juice to put in Titania's eyes, but he also sends Puck to put some in Demetrius' eyes so when he awakens he will see Helena and love her. Puck has never seen Demetrius, so King Oberon tells him he will recognize the man by the Athenian style of clothing he is wearing.

❑ Distribute a copy of the script to each student who can read.

❑ (Optional) Take a sneak peek at these lines from the script and enjoy Shakespeare's wording.

> » Lines 2–6 are a fairy's description of where it has been.
>
>> Over hill, over dale,
>>   Thorough bush, thorough brier,
>> Over park, over pale,
>>   Thorough flood, thorough fire,
>> I do wander everywhere,

» Lines 32–42: You can learn about Puck's mischievous tendencies (and his formal name) in this fairy's description of what others say about him.

> Either I mistake your shape and making quite,
> Or else you are that shrewd and knavish sprite
> Call'd Robin Goodfellow: are not you he
> That frights the maidens of the villagery;
> Skim milk, and sometimes labour in the quern
> And bootless make the breathless housewife churn;
> And sometime make the drink to bear no barm;
> Mislead night-wanderers, laughing at their harm?
> Those that Hobgoblin call you, and sweet Puck,
> You do their work, and they shall have good luck:
> Are not you he?

» Line 60: Since Oberon is not happy to meet his queen that night, he greets her with "Ill met by moonlight, proud Titania."

» Line 175–176: When Oberon sends Puck to fetch the magical flower, and do it quickly, Puck assures him:

> I'll put a girdle round about the earth
> In forty minutes.

» Lines 176–185 detail Oberon's plan with the magical flower's juice.

> Having once this juice,
> I'll watch Titania when she is asleep,
> And drop the liquor of it in her eyes.
> The next thing then she waking looks upon,
> Be it on lion, bear, or wolf, or bull,
> On meddling monkey, or on busy ape,
> She shall pursue it with the soul of love:
> And ere I take this charm from off her sight,
> As I can take it with another herb,
> I'll make her render up her page to me.

» Lines 249–256 beautifully describe a place full of flowers where Titania likes to go to sleep.

> I know a bank where the wild thyme blows,
> Where oxlips and the nodding violet grows,
> Quite over-canopied with luscious woodbine,

Notes

With sweet musk-roses and with eglantine:
There sleeps Titania sometime of the night,
Lull'd in these flowers with dances and delight;
And there the snake throws her enamell'd skin,
Weed wide enough to wrap a fairy in:

❑ Listen to Act II, Scene 1, on the audio dramatization (approx. 17 minutes) and follow along in the script, or assign students to read aloud the various characters' lines themselves. If you are assigning students to read aloud, the following list might be helpful; it details the characters who speak and the approximate number of lines each one has in this scene.

- Puck, special follower of the fairy king (37 lines)
- Fairy, one of the fairy queen's followers (28 lines)
- Oberon, king of the fairies (79 lines)
- Titania, queen of the fairies (72 lines)
- Demetrius, young man who wants to marry Hermia (23 lines)
- Helena, young woman who loves Demetrius (34 lines)

Act II, Scene 2

Notes

❑ Ask students what they recall from last time's reading about Oberon, the fairy king, and his plans for using the juice of the magical flower. Explain that today they will listen to how well those plans succeed in Act II, Scene 2. Read the scene summary to give students the context for the lines they will be hearing.

Scene Summary: Oberon and Puck begin to carry out their plan to unite Demetrius and Helena and to put Titania in a ridiculous position. Oberon is successful in anointing Titania's eyes with the flower juice, but Puck mistakenly puts the juice on Lysander's eyes. When Lysander awakens, he sees Helena first and, so, abandons Hermia.

❑ Distribute a copy of the script to each student who can read.

❑ (Optional) Take a sneak peek at these lines from the script and enjoy Shakespeare's wording.

» Lines 27–34: As Oberon squeezes the flower's juice on Titania's eyelids, he describes what sort of creature he hopes she will see, and thus love, when she wakes up.

> What thou seest when thou dost wake,
> Do it for thy true-love take,
> Love and languish for his sake:
> Be it ounce, or cat, or bear,
> Pard, or boar with bristled hair,
> In thy eye that shall appear
> When thou wakest, it is thy dear:
> Wake when some vile thing is near.

» Line 52: Lysander uses *lying* and *lie* in the same line but with two meanings. He is speaking of lying on the ground and assuring Hermia that he is telling the truth, not a lie: "For lying so, Hermia, I do not lie."

» Lines 123–128: Helena thinks Lysander is mocking her with his sudden profession of love.

> Wherefore was I to this keen mockery born?
> When at your hands did I deserve this scorn?
> Is't not enough, is't not enough, young man,

Notes

> That I did never, no, nor never can,
> Deserve a sweet look from Demetrius' eye,
> But you must flout my insufficiency?

☐ Listen to Act II, Scene 2, on the audio dramatization (approx. 12 minutes) and follow along in the script, or assign students to read aloud the various characters' lines themselves. If you are assigning students to read aloud, the following list might be helpful; it details the characters who speak and the approximate number of lines each one has in this scene.

- Titania, queen of the fairies (8 lines)
- First Fairy (8 lines, singing)
- Chorus of fairies (14 lines, singing)
- Second Fairy (2 lines)
- Oberon, king of the fairies (8 lines)
- Lysander, Hermia's true love who becomes enamored with Helena (44 lines)
- Hermia, young woman who loves Lysander (26 lines)
- Puck, special follower of the fairy king (18 lines)
- Demetrius, young man who wants to marry Hermia (2 lines)
- Helena, young woman who loves Demetrius (32 lines)

Act III, Scene 1

❑ Ask students what they recall from last time's reading about Oberon and Puck's use of the juice of the magical flower. Explain that today they will rejoin the troupe of would-be actors as they meet in the woods to rehearse amidst the mixed-up lovers and mischievous fairies in Act III, Scene 1. Read the scene summary to give students the context for the lines they will be hearing.

> *Scene Summary:* Puck listens as the bumbling would-be actors work out the perceived difficulties in their script. When Nick Bottom exits the scene, Puck takes the opportunity to pop a donkey's head onto his shoulders. Nick is oblivious to the change in his appearance and thinks his fellow actors are teasing when they all flee in fear.
>
> Titania, the fairy queen, is sleeping nearby. The commotion wakes her, and the first living creature she sees is Nick Bottom with the donkey's head. Because of the magical flower juice, she immediately professes her love and calls on her fairy followers to make Nick comfortable.

❑ Distribute a copy of the script to each student who can read.

❑ (Optional) Take a sneak peek at these lines from the script and enjoy Shakespeare's wording.

» Lines 21–24: Quince and Bottom debate how many syllables to include in the lines of the prologue they will write. A line of eight syllables followed by a line of six is a common format for a ballad.

>   QUINCE: Well, we will have such a prologue; and it shall
>   be written in eight and six.
>
>   BOTTOM: No, make it two more; let it be written in eight
>   and eight.

» Lines 138–139: When Titania expresses that she loves the donkey-headed Nick Bottom at first sight, his reply points out the turn of events that occurs during these middle acts of the play: "reason and love keep little company together now-a-days."

» Line 201: After Nick Bottom stumblingly greets the fairies, Titania, even in her love-sick state, realizes it is better when he does not talk; so she tells her fairies to "Tie up my love's tongue, bring him silently."

Notes

Notes

❏ Listen to Act III, Scene 1, on the audio dramatization (approx. 13 minutes) and follow along in the script, or assign students to read aloud the various characters' lines themselves. If you are assigning students to read aloud, the following list might be helpful; it details the characters who speak and the approximate number of lines each one has in this scene.

- Bottom, a vain and somewhat dimwitted actor (87 lines)
- Quince, director of the troupe (34 lines)
- Snout, actor (10 lines)
- Flute, actor (8 lines)
- Starveling, actor (3 lines)
- Puck, special follower of the fairy king (11 lines)
- Titania, queen of the fairies (34 lines)
- Peaseblossom, fairy (4 lines)
- Cobweb, fairy (4 lines)
- Moth, fairy (3 lines)
- Mustardseed, fairy (4 lines)

Act III, Scene 2

❑ Ask students what they recall from last time's reading about the actors' rehearsing in the woods. Explain that today they will listen to Act III, Scene 2, in which things come to a head as Oberon and Puck discover they made a mistake. Read the scene summary to give students the context for the lines they will be hearing.

Scene Summary: Puck returns to Oberon to report on Titania's fate: loving the actor with the donkey's head. They both think it a fitting joke. But presently they discover Puck's mistake of putting the flower juice on Lysander's eyes. To set things right again, they watch until Demetrius sleeps; then Oberon puts some of the juice on his eyes and Puck quickly fetches Helena so Demetrius will see her when he awakes.

The scheme works, but now both young men are indifferent to Hermia and enamored with Helena, who thinks they are all mocking her. Eventually the two men challenge each other to a duel to prove which of them loves Helena most. Puck is enjoying their confusion, but Oberon sends him to make sure the two men do not hurt each other.

Puck is to overhang the sky with fog, and by mimicking the men's voices to each other, lead them separate directions into the woods until they grow weary and sleep. Then he can put the antidote herb on Lysander's eyes so he will revert to loving Hermia. In the meantime, Oberon will go to the queen and try once again to gain the little page-boy from her before he puts the antidote on her eyes.

❑ Distribute a copy of the script to each student who can read.

❑ (Optional) Take a sneak peek at these lines from the script and enjoy Shakespeare's wording.

» Lines 100–101: A fun reply to use when sent on an errand:
   I go, I go; look how I go,
   Swifter than arrow from the Tartar's bow.

» Lines 110–115: When Puck sees Lysander pleading with Helena, he is amused at the spectacle. The final line is an oft-quoted one.
   Captain of our fairy band,
   Helena is here at hand;
   And the youth, mistook by me,

Notes

This is a long scene, close to 30 minutes; feel free to divide it between two sittings if desired.

> Pleading for a lover's fee.
> Shall we their fond pageant see?
> Lord, what fools these mortals be!

» Lines 461–463: Puck announces what the effect of their scheme this time will be:
> Jack shall have Jill;
> Nought shall go ill;
> The man shall have his mare again, and all shall be well.

❑ Listen to Act III, Scene 2, on the audio dramatization (split scene: approx. 7 minutes on the first disc and 20 on the second disc) and follow along in the script, or assign students to read aloud the various characters' lines themselves. If you are assigning students to read aloud, the following list might be helpful; it details the characters who speak and the approximate number of lines each one has in this scene.

- Oberon (63 lines)
- Puck (100 lines)
- Hermia (80 lines)
- Demetrius (61 lines)
- Lysander (60 lines)
- Helena (116 lines)

Act IV, Scene 1

❑ Ask students what they recall from last time's reading about how Oberon and Puck discover their mistakes and set about to make them right. Explain that today, in Act IV, Scene 1, things will finally get straightened out. Read the scene summary to give students the context for the lines they will be hearing.

Scene Summary: Oberon secures the page-boy from Titania; then while Nick Bottom and Titania are asleep, he puts the antidote on Titania's eyes and Puck removes the donkey head from Nick. When Titania awakes, she and Oberon reconcile their differences and agree to dance at the Duke's wedding.

The Duke, Hermia's father, and others of the court enter the woods as a hunting party and find the four lovers asleep. The Duke remembers that this is the day Hermia is supposed to give her answer, so they awaken all four young people, marveling that the two rival young men can sleep so peacefully in the same area. Lysander confesses their plot to escape to his aunt's in order to marry. Egeus seizes upon this information as sufficient evidence to bring down the law on them. However, Demetrius explains that he no longer wants to marry Hermia; he used to be betrothed to Helena and now he loves her again. Theseus overrules Egeus' complaint and promises that the two couples will be married at the same time as he and Hippolyta.

The dazed couples have a hard time comprehending all that has happened, not sure what was real and what seems to be a dream. Nick Bottom awakens quite confused, as well, and comes up with the idea that Quince must write a ballad based on his strange dream.

❑ Distribute a copy of the script to each student who can read.

❑ (Optional) Take a sneak peek at these lines from the script and enjoy Shakespeare's wording.

» Lines 61–68: Once Oberon gets possession of the page-boy, he puts the antidote on his queen's eyelids, tells Puck to remove the ass's head from Nick Bottom, and details his expectations for everyone involved in the fairy magic of the night.

> And now I have the boy, I will undo
> This hateful imperfection of her eyes:
> And, gentle Puck, take this transformed scalp
> From off the head of this Athenian swain;
> That, he awaking when the other do,
> May all to Athens back again repair

Notes

Make arrangements now for students to watch a performance of the play at the end of your study. See page 34 for details.

Notes

        And think no more of this night's accidents
        But as the fierce vexation of a dream.

» Lines 92–93: Puck's warning that morning has come:
    Fairy king, attend, and mark:
    I do hear the morning lark.

» Lines 172–175: Demetrius' profession of his re-kindled love for Helena:
    But, like in sickness, did I loathe this food;
    But, as in health, come to my natural taste,
    Now I do wish it, love it, long for it,
    And will for evermore be true to it.

» Lines 209–212: An example of Nick Bottom's "sharp wit" as he mixes his words:
    The eye of man hath not heard, the
    ear of man hath not seen, man's hand is not able to
    taste, his tongue to conceive, nor his heart to report,
    what my dream was.

❏ Listen to Act IV, Scene 1, on the audio dramatization (approx. 15 minutes) and follow along in the script, or assign students to read aloud the various characters' lines themselves. If you are assigning students to read aloud, the following list might be helpful; it details the characters who speak and the approximate number of lines each one has in this scene.

- Titania (23 lines)
- Nick Bottom (47 lines)
- Peaseblossom (1 line)
- Cobweb (1 line)
- Mustardseed (2 lines)
- Oberon (46 lines)
- Puck (3 lines)
- Theseus (41 lines)
- Hippolyta (7 lines)
- Egeus (11 lines)
- Lysander (10 lines)
- Demetrius (24 lines)
- Hermia (3 lines)
- Helena (4 lines)

Act IV, Scene 2

- Ask students what they recall from last time's reading about how the night ended for the fairy king and queen, the couples of young people, and the actor Nick. Explain that today they will hear the actors preparing for their play in Act IV, Scene 2. Read the scene summary to give students the context for the lines they will be hearing.

    Scene Summary: As the time draws near, the other actors are on the outlook for Nick Bottom and not sure what has happened to him. At the last minute he appears, eager to relate his strange experiences but carried along with the preparations at hand. From all the presentations offered for the wedding celebration, the Duke has selected their play and they must get ready to perform.

- Distribute a copy of the script to each student who can read.

- (Optional) Take a sneak peek at these lines from the script and enjoy Shakespeare's wording.

    » Lines 5–6: Flute is worried that the play will be ruined and the show cannot go on since they cannot find Nick Bottom:

    > If he come not, then the play is marred: it goes
    > not forward, doth it?

    » Lines 33–42: Nick gives final advice to his fellow actors as they get ready to perform:

    > Get your apparel together,
    > good strings to your beards, new ribbands to your
    > pumps; meet presently at the palace; every man look
    > o'er his part; for the short and the long is, our play is
    > preferred. In any case, let Thisby have clean linen; and
    > let not him that plays the lion pare his nails, for they
    > shall hang out for the lion's claws. And, most dear
    > actors, eat no onions nor garlic, for we are to utter sweet
    > breath; and I do not doubt but to hear them say, it is a
    > sweet comedy. No more words: away! go, away!

- Listen to Act IV, Scene 2, on the audio dramatization (approx. 3 minutes) and follow along in the script, or assign students to read aloud the various characters' lines themselves. If you are assigning students to read aloud, the following list might be

---

Notes

This scene is very short. You may combine it with Act V, but keep in mind that Act V is already 30 minutes long by itself.

"Ribands" is an old form of "ribbons"; "pumps" are light shoes.

Notes

helpful; it details the characters who speak and the approximate number of lines each one has in this scene.

- Quince (9 lines)
- Starveling (2 lines)
- Flute (12 lines)
- Snug (4 lines)
- Bottom (15 lines)

Act V

- ❑ Ask students what they recall from last time's reading about the actors' preparing to perform. Explain that today they will listen to the final scene, Act V, in which they will witness the troupe's performance at the Duke's wedding celebration. Read the scene summary to give students the context for the lines they will be hearing.

    Scene Summary: Theseus looks over the list of possible entertainments and chooses the play of Pyramus and Thisby. As the troupe performs their play, those in the audience make side comments and enjoy the spectacle immensely. The kingdom of fairies makes an appearance to bless the happy couples. Last, Puck comes forth to deliver the epilogue, saying that if we don't like the play, we can tell ourselves that we were dreaming.

- ❑ Distribute a copy of the script to each student who can read.

- ❑ (Optional) Take a sneak peek at these lines from the script and enjoy Shakespeare's wording.

    » Lines 7–22: Upon hearing the account of what happened to the four young people in the woods last night, the Duke attributes it to the strong powers of imagination.

    > The lunatic, the lover and the poet
    > Are of imagination all compact:
    > One sees more devils than vast hell can hold,
    > That is, the madman: the lover, all as frantic,
    > Sees Helen's beauty in a brow of Egypt:
    > The poet's eye, in fine frenzy rolling,
    > Doth glance from heaven to earth, from earth to heaven;
    > And as imagination bodies forth
    > The forms of things unknown, the poet's pen
    > Turns them to shapes and gives to airy nothing
    > A local habitation and a name.
    > Such tricks hath strong imagination,
    > That if it would but apprehend some joy,
    > It comprehends some bringer of that joy;
    > Or in the night, imagining some fear,
    > How easy is a bush supposed a bear!

Notes

» Lines 61–70: Philostrate explains how the troupe's play is brief yet tedious and tragical yet merry.

> A play there is, my lord, some ten words long,
> Which is as brief as I have known a play;
> But by ten words, my lord, it is too long,
> Which makes it tedious; for in all the play
> There is not one word apt, one player fitted:
> And tragical, my noble lord, it is;
> For Pyramus therein doth kill himself.
> Which, when I saw rehearsed, I must confess,
> Made mine eyes water; but more merry tears
> The passion of loud laughter never shed.

» Lines 108–117: By rearranging the punctuation ("points"), Shakespeare has switched the meaning of the whole prologue, reflecting how Quince reads it incorrectly. Try moving the punctuation to different places to form sentences that convey a complimentary prologue, rather than an insulting one. For example, "If we offend, it is with our good will that you should think we come not to offend, but with good will to show our simple skill."

> If we offend, it is with our good will.
>   That you should think, we come not to offend,
> But with good will. To show our simple skill,
>   That is the true beginning of our end.
> Consider then we come but in despite.
>   We do not come as minding to contest you,
> Our true intent is. All for your delight
>   We are not here. That you should here repent you,
> The actors are at hand and by their show
> You shall know all that you are like to know.

» Lines 355–356: Theseus announces that the clock has struck midnight and it is almost time for the fairies to emerge:

> The iron tongue of midnight hath told twelve:
> Lovers, to bed; 'tis almost fairy time.

» Lines 415–420: Puck suggests to the audience that what they just witnessed was also a dream:

> If we shadows have offended,
> Think but this, and all is mended,

> That you have but slumber'd here
> While these visions did appear.
>   And this weak and idle theme,
>   No more yielding but a dream,

- ❏ Listen to Act V on the audio dramatization (approx. 31 minutes) and follow along in the script, or assign students to read aloud the various characters' lines themselves. If you are assigning students to read aloud, the following list might be helpful; it details the characters who speak and the approximate number of lines each one has in this scene.

  - Hippolyta (23 lines)
  - Theseus (130 lines)
  - Philostrate (24 lines)
  - Lysander (12 lines)
  - Demetrius (24 lines)
  - Quince, giving the prologue (35 lines)
  - Starveling, playing the part of the moonshine (6 lines)
  - Snout, playing the part of the wall (12 lines)
  - Flute, playing the part of Thisby (34 lines)
  - Snug, playing the part of the lion (9 lines)
  - Bottom, playing the part of Pyramus (57 lines)
  - Puck (36 lines)
  - Oberon (28 lines)
  - Titania (4 lines)

Notes

This is a long scene, close to 30 minutes; feel free to divide it between two sittings if desired.

Notes

Be sure to do your research to avoid any unpleasant surprises when watching Shakespeare productions. Unfortunately, some directors feel compelled to add unnecessary visual elaborations on the text. Preview any video presentation and check with someone who is directly involved with any live production to find out how it aligns with the original script and how appropriate it is for children.

Step 3: Watch the play.

Now that you and your students are familiar with the story line and the script, you are ready for the best part of this study: watch a presentation of the play! Check for any local live performances that you could attend, or watch a video recording. (See video reviews below.)

Video Recording Reviews

- The 1935 adaptation produced by Warner Brothers Pictures is very suitable for children. It features James Cagney, Olivia de Havilland, and Mickey Rooney among others. Note that it is an adaptation; not all lines are spoken, not all scenes are exact. But it highlights the comedy and the fantasy elements with plenty of fairies, sprites, nymphs, elves, and gnomes. It also features many musical pieces. Felix Mendelssohn composed music for a production of *A Midsummer Night's Dream* during his lifetime, including his famous "Wedding March." Some of Mendelssohn's music has been re-orchestrated and woven into this 1935 adaptation. *(Approx. 143 minutes)*

- The 1981 BBC version directed by Elijah Moshinsky is more faithful to the original script, but the performance has a serious tone to it—at times almost bordering on sinister—that doesn't give it the feel of a comedy. It does introduce the idea that lines do not have to be spoken in solo fashion; some of the dialogue in the forest is delivered with two, three, or even four of the young lovers all talking at once. *(Approx. 112 minutes)*

- The 1969 Royal Shakespeare Company version by Peter Hall is adapted and has a definite '60s feel. One example is that it features girls in mini skirts. *(Approx. 124 minutes)*

- The 1999 version directed by Michael Hoffman, starring Kevin Kline and Michelle Pfeiffer, is rated PG-13. Parental advisories include sexual innuendos and nudity. The fairies appear drunk in the first scene. *(Approx. 116 minutes)*

- In the 1996 version, directed and written by Adrian Noble, a modern-day boy dreams the play. The DVD release of this performance is rated PG-13. Parental advisories include sexual content, particularly in the scene between Titania and Bottom. *(Approx. 105 minutes)*

A Midsummer Night's Dream

Notes

Act I, Scene 1
Setting: Athens, the palace of Theseus.
Enter Theseus, Hippolyta, Philostrate, with Attendants.

THESEUS
    Now, fair Hippolyta, our nuptial hour
    Draws on apace; four happy days bring in
    Another moon: but, O, methinks, how slow
    This old moon wanes! She lingers my desires,
    Like to a step-dame or a dowager   5
    Long withering out a young man's revenue.

This is the Theseus who fought the mythical Minotaur.

HIPPOLYTA
    Four days will quickly steep themselves in night;
    Four nights will quickly dream away the time;
    And then the moon, like to a silver bow
    New-bent in heaven, shall behold the night   10
    Of our solemnities.

THESEUS   Go, Philostrate,
    Stir up the Athenian youth to merriments;
    Awake the pert and nimble spirit of mirth;
    Turn melancholy forth to funerals;
    The pale companion is not for our pomp.   15
    Exit Philostrate.
    Hippolyta, I woo'd thee with my sword,
    And won thy love, doing thee injuries;
    But I will wed thee in another key,
    With pomp, with triumph and with revelling.
    Enter Egeus, Hermia, Lysander, and Demetrius.

Sometimes Shakespeare would split a line of poetry between two characters. Theseus' first line here finishes Hippolyta's previous line, so it is moved to the right to visually show that completion.

EGEUS
    Happy be Theseus, our renowned duke!   20

THESEUS
    Thanks, good Egeus: what's the news with thee?

EGEUS
    Full of vexation come I, with complaint
    Against my child, my daughter Hermia.

Notes

    Stand forth, Demetrius. My noble lord,
    This man hath my consent to marry her. 25
    Stand forth, Lysander: and my gracious duke,
    This hath bewitched the bosom of my child;
    Thou, thou, Lysander, thou hast given her rhymes,
    And interchanged love-tokens with my child:
    Thou hast by moonlight at her window sung, 30
    With feigning voice verses of feigning love,
    And stolen the impression of her fantasy
    With bracelets of thy hair, rings, gauds, conceits,
    Knacks, trifles, nosegays, sweetmeats—messengers
    Of strong prevailment in unhardened youth: 35
    With cunning hast thou filched my daughter's heart,
    Turned her obedience, which is due to me,
    To stubborn harshness: and, my gracious duke,
    Be it so she will not here before your grace
    Consent to marry with Demetrius, 40
    I beg the ancient privilege of Athens,
    As she is mine, I may dispose of her:
    Which shall be either to this gentleman
    Or to her death, according to our law
    Immediately provided in that case. 45

THESEUS
    What say you, Hermia? Be advised, fair maid:
    To you your father should be as a god;
    One that composed your beauties, yea, and one
    To whom you are but as a form in wax
    By him imprinted and within his power 50
    To leave the figure or disfigure it.
    Demetrius is a worthy gentleman.

HERMIA
    So is Lysander.

THESEUS   In himself he is;
    But in this kind, wanting your father's voice,
    The other must be held the worthier. 55

HERMIA
    I would my father looked but with my eyes.

THESEUS
    Rather your eyes must with his judgment look.

HERMIA
    I do entreat your grace to pardon me.
    I know not by what power I am made bold,
    Nor how it may concern my modesty,   60
    In such a presence here to plead my thoughts;
    But I beseech your grace that I may know
    The worst that may befall me in this case,
    If I refuse to wed Demetrius.

THESEUS
    Either to die the death or to abjure   65
    For ever the society of men.
    Therefore, fair Hermia, question your desires;
    Know of your youth, examine well your blood,
    Whether, if you yield not to your father's choice,
    You can endure the livery of a nun,   70
    For aye to be in shady cloister mewed,
    To live a barren sister all your life,
    Chanting faint hymns to the cold fruitless moon.
    Thrice-blessed they that master so their blood,
    To undergo such maiden pilgrimage;   75
    But earthlier happy is the rose distilled,
    Than that which withering on the virgin thorn
    Grows, lives and dies in single blessedness.

HERMIA
    So will I grow, so live, so die, my lord,
    Ere I will yield my virgin patent up   80
    Unto his lordship, whose unwished yoke
    My soul consents not to give sovereignty.

THESEUS
    Take time to pause; and, by the next new moon—
    The sealing-day betwixt my love and me,
    For everlasting bond of fellowship—   85
    Upon that day either prepare to die
    For disobedience to your father's will,
    Or else to wed Demetrius, as he would;
    Or on Diana's altar to protest
    For aye austerity and single life.   90

DEMETRIUS
    Relent, sweet Hermia: and, Lysander, yield

Notes

Thy crazed title to my certain right.

LYSANDER
You have her father's love, Demetrius;
Let me have Hermia's: do you marry him.

EGEUS
Scornful Lysander! true, he hath my love, 95
And what is mine my love shall render him.
And she is mine, and all my right of her
I do estate unto Demetrius.

LYSANDER
I am, my lord, as well derived as he,
As well possessed; my love is more than his; 100
My fortunes every way as fairly ranked,
If not with vantage, as Demetrius';
And, which is more than all these boasts can be,
I am beloved of beauteous Hermia:
Why should not I then prosecute my right? 105
Demetrius—I'll avouch it to his head—
Made love to Nedar's daughter, Helena,
And won her soul; and she, sweet lady, dotes,
Devoutly dotes, dotes in idolatry,
Upon this spotted and inconstant man. 110

THESEUS
I must confess that I have heard so much,
And with Demetrius thought to have spoke thereof;
But, being over-full of self-affairs,
My mind did lose it. But, Demetrius, come;
And come, Egeus; you shall go with me, 115
I have some private schooling for you both.
For you, fair Hermia, look you arm yourself
To fit your fancies to your father's will;
Or else the law of Athens yields you up—
Which by no means we may extenuate— 120
To death, or to a vow of single life.
Come, my Hippolyta: what cheer, my love?
Demetrius and Egeus, go along:
I must employ you in some business
Against our nuptial and confer with you 125
Of something nearly that concerns yourselves.

EGEUS
    With duty and desire we follow you.
        Exeunt all but Lysander and Hermia.

LYSANDER
    How now, my love! Why is your cheek so pale?
    How chance the roses there do fade so fast?

HERMIA
    Belike for want of rain, which I could well   130
    Beteem them from the tempest of my eyes.

LYSANDER
    Ay me! for aught that I could ever read,
    Could ever hear by tale or history,
    The course of true love never did run smooth;
    But either it was different in blood,—   135

HERMIA
    O cross! too high to be enthralled to low.

LYSANDER
    Or else misgraffed in respect of years,—

HERMIA
    O spite! too old to be engaged to young.

LYSANDER
    Or merit stood upon the choice of friends,—

HERMIA
    O hell! to choose love by another's eyes.   140

LYSANDER
    Or, if there were a sympathy in choice,
    War, death, or sickness did lay siege to it,
    Making it momentany as a sound,
    Swift as a shadow, short as any dream;
    Brief as the lightning in the collied night,   145
    That, in a spleen, unfolds both heaven and earth,
    And ere a man hath power to say "Behold!"
    The jaws of darkness do devour it up:
    So quick bright things come to confusion.

HERMIA
    If then true lovers have been ever crossed,   150

It stands as an edict in destiny:
Then let us teach our trial patience,
Because it is a customary cross,
As due to love as thoughts and dreams and sighs,
Wishes and tears, poor fancy's followers. 155

LYSANDER
A good persuasion: therefore, hear me, Hermia.
I have a widow aunt, a dowager
Of great revenue, and she hath no child:
From Athens is her house remote seven leagues;
And she respects me as her only son. 160
There, gentle Hermia, may I marry thee;
And to that place the sharp Athenian law
Cannot pursue us. If thou lovest me then,
Steal forth thy father's house to-morrow night;
And in the wood, a league without the town, 165
Where I did meet thee once with Helena,
To do observance to a morn of May,
There will I stay for thee.

HERMIA   My good Lysander!
I swear to thee, by Cupid's strongest bow,
By his best arrow with the golden head, 170
By the simplicity of Venus' doves,
By that which knitteth souls and prospers loves,
And by that fire which burned the Carthage queen,
When the false Troyan under sail was seen,
By all the vows that ever men have broke, 175
In number more than ever women spoke,
In that same place thou hast appointed me,
To-morrow truly will I meet with thee.

LYSANDER
Keep promise, love. Look, here comes Helena.
  Enter Helena.

HERMIA
God speed fair Helena! Whither away? 180

HELENA
Call you me fair? That "fair" again unsay.
Demetrius loves your fair: O happy fair!

Your eyes are lode-stars; and your tongue's sweet air
More tuneable than lark to shepherd's ear,
When wheat is green, when hawthorn buds appear. 185
Sickness is catching: O, were favour so,
Yours would I catch, fair Hermia, ere I go;
My ear should catch your voice, my eye your eye,
My tongue should catch your tongue's sweet melody.
Were the world mine, Demetrius being bated, 190
The rest I'd give to be to you translated.
O, teach me how you look, and with what art
You sway the motion of Demetrius' heart.

HERMIA
I frown upon him, yet he loves me still.

HELENA
O that your frowns would teach my smiles such skill! 195

HERMIA
I give him curses, yet he gives me love.

HELENA
O that my prayers could such affection move!

HERMIA
The more I hate, the more he follows me.

HELENA
The more I love, the more he hateth me.

HERMIA
His folly, Helena, is no fault of mine. 200

HELENA
None, but your beauty: would that fault were mine!

HERMIA
Take comfort: he no more shall see my face;
Lysander and myself will fly this place.
Before the time I did Lysander see,
Seemed Athens as a paradise to me: 205
O, then, what graces in my love do dwell,
That he hath turned a heaven unto a hell!

LYSANDER
Helen, to you our minds we will unfold:

Notes

    To-morrow night, when Phoebe doth behold
    Her silver visage in the watery glass,   210
    Decking with liquid pearl the bladed grass,
    A time that lovers' flights doth still conceal,
    Through Athens' gates have we devised to steal.

HERMIA
    And in the wood, where often you and I
    Upon faint primrose-beds were wont to lie,   215
    Emptying our bosoms of their counsel sweet,
    There my Lysander and myself shall meet;
    And thence from Athens turn away our eyes,
    To seek new friends and stranger companies.
    Farewell, sweet playfellow: pray thou for us;   220
    And good luck grant thee thy Demetrius!
    Keep word, Lysander: we must starve our sight
    From lovers' food till morrow deep midnight.

LYSANDER
    I will, my Hermia.
    Exit Hermia.
                      Helena, adieu:
    As you on him, Demetrius dote on you.   225
    Exit Lysander.

HELENA
    How happy some o'er other some can be!
    Through Athens I am thought as fair as she.
    But what of that? Demetrius thinks not so;
    He will not know what all but he do know:
    And as he errs, doting on Hermia's eyes,   230
    So I, admiring of his qualities:
    Things base and vile, folding no quantity,
    Love can transpose to form and dignity:
    Love looks not with the eyes, but with the mind;
    And therefore is winged Cupid painted blind: 235
    Nor hath Love's mind of any judgment taste;
    Wings and no eyes figure unheedy haste:
    And therefore is Love said to be a child,
    Because in choice he is so oft beguiled.
    As waggish boys in game themselves forswear,   240
    So the boy Love is perjured everywhere:

For ere Demetrius looked on Hermia's eyne,
He hailed down oaths that he was only mine;
And when this hail some heat from Hermia felt,
So he dissolved, and showers of oaths did melt. 245
I will go tell him of fair Hermia's flight:
Then to the wood will he to-morrow night
Pursue her; and for this intelligence
If I have thanks, it is a dear expense:
But herein mean I to enrich my pain, 250
To have his sight thither and back again.
   Exit Helena.

Notes

Act I, Scene 2

Setting: Athens, Quince's house.
Enter Quince, Snug, Bottom, Flute, Snout, and Starveling.

> QUINCE: Is all our company here?
>
> BOTTOM: You were best to call them generally, man by man, according to the scrip.
>
> QUINCE: Here is the scroll of every man's name which is thought fit, through all Athens, to play in our interlude before the duke and the duchess on his wedding-day at night.   5
>
> BOTTOM: First, good Peter Quince, say what the play treats on, then read the names of the actors, and so grow to a point.   10
>
> QUINCE: Marry, our play is, "The most lamentable comedy, and most cruel death of Pyramus and Thisby."
>
> BOTTOM: A very good piece of work, I assure you, and a merry. Now, good Peter Quince, call forth your actors by the scroll. Masters, spread yourselves.   15
>
> QUINCE: Answer as I call you. Nick Bottom, the weaver.
>
> BOTTOM: Ready. Name what part I am for, and proceed.
>
> QUINCE: You, Nick Bottom, are set down for Pyramus.
>
> BOTTOM: What is Pyramus? a lover, or a tyrant?
>
> QUINCE: A lover, that kills himself most gallant for love.   20
>
> BOTTOM: That will ask some tears in the true performing of it: if I do it, let the audience look to their eyes; I will move storms, I will condole in some measure. To the rest: yet my chief humour is for a tyrant: I could play Ercles rarely, or a part to tear a cat in, to make all split.   25
>
> > The raging rocks
> > And shivering shocks
> > Shall break the locks
> >   Of prison gates;
> > And Phibbus' car   30
> > Shall shine from far
> > And make and mar

Notes

Shakespeare wrote the lines of his plays in both prose (conversational speaking) and poetry.

PERSON: *Prose lines will look like this.*

PERSON
Poetry lines will look like this.

"Ercles" refers to Hercules.

       The foolish Fates.
  This was lofty! Now name the rest of the players. This is
    Ercles' vein, a tyrant's vein; a lover is more condoling.   35

QUINCE: Francis Flute, the bellows-mender.

FLUTE: Here, Peter Quince.

QUINCE: Flute, you must take Thisby on you.

FLUTE: What is Thisby? a wandering knight?

QUINCE: It is the lady that Pyramus must love.   40

FLUTE: Nay, faith, let me not play a woman; I have a
    beard coming.

QUINCE: That's all one: you shall play it in a mask,
    and you may speak as small as you will.

BOTTOM: An I may hide my face, let me play Thisby   45
    too. I'll speak in a monstrous little voice.
    "Thisne, Thisne;" "Ah, Pyramus, lover dear!
    thy Thisby dear, and lady dear!"

QUINCE: No, no; you must play Pyramus: and, Flute, you
    Thisby.   50

BOTTOM: Well, proceed.

QUINCE: Robin Starveling, the tailor.

STARVELING: Here, Peter Quince.

QUINCE: Robin Starveling, you must play Thisby's mother.
    Tom Snout, the tinker.   55

SNOUT: Here, Peter Quince.

QUINCE: You, Pyramus' father: myself, Thisby's father:
    Snug, the joiner, you, the lion's part: and, I hope,
    here is a play fitted.

SNUG: Have you the lion's part written? Pray you,   60
    if it be, give it me, for I am slow of study.

QUINCE: You may do it extempore, for it is nothing but
    roaring.

BOTTOM: Let me play the lion too: I will roar, that I will

Notes

Notes

do any man's heart good to hear me; I will roar, that I will make the duke say "Let him roar again, let him roar again."

QUINCE: An you should do it too terribly, you would fright the duchess and the ladies, that they would shriek; and that were enough to hang us all.

ALL: That would hang us, every mother's son.

BOTTOM: I grant you, friends, if you should fright the ladies out of their wits, they would have no more discretion but to hang us: but I will aggravate my voice so that I will roar you as gently as any sucking dove; I will roar you an 'twere any nightingale.

QUINCE: You can play no part but Pyramus; for Pyramus is a sweet-faced man; a proper man, as one shall see in a summer's day; a most lovely gentleman-like man: therefore you must needs play Pyramus.

BOTTOM: Well, I will undertake it. What beard were I best to play it in?

QUINCE: Why, what you will.

BOTTOM: I will discharge it in either your straw-colour beard, your orange-tawny beard, your purple-in-grain beard, or your French-crown-colour beard, your perfit yellow.

QUINCE: Some of your French crowns have no hair at all, and then you will play bare-faced. But, masters, here are your parts: and I am to entreat you, request you and desire you, to con them by to-morrow night; and meet me in the palace wood, a mile without the town, by moonlight; there will we rehearse, for if we meet in the city, we shall be dogged with company, and our devices known. In the meantime I will draw a bill of properties, such as our play wants. I pray you, fail me not.

BOTTOM: We will meet; and there we may rehearse most obscenely and courageously. Take pains; be perfit: adieu.

QUINCE: At the duke's oak we meet.

BOTTOM: Enough; hold or cut bow-strings. 100
Exeunt.

Notes

Notes

Act II, Scene 1

Setting: A wood near Athens.
Enter, from opposite sides, a Fairy and Puck.

PUCK
    How now, spirit! whither wander you?

FAIRY
          Over hill, over dale,
              Thorough bush, thorough brier,
          Over park, over pale,
              Thorough flood, thorough fire,   5
    I do wander everywhere,
    Swifter than the moon's sphere;
    And I serve the fairy queen,
    To dew her orbs upon the green.
    The cowslips tall her pensioners be: 10
    In their gold coats spots you see;
    Those be rubies, fairy favours,
    In those freckles live their savours:
    I must go seek some dewdrops here
    And hang a pearl in every cowslip's ear.   15
    Farewell, thou lob of spirits; I'll be gone:
    Our queen and all our elves come here anon.

PUCK
    The king doth keep his revels here to-night:
    Take heed the queen come not within his sight;
    For Oberon is passing fell and wrath,   20
    Because that she as her attendant hath
    A lovely boy, stolen from an Indian king;
    She never had so sweet a changeling;
    And jealous Oberon would have the child
    Knight of his train, to trace the forests wild;   25
    But she perforce withholds the loved boy,
    Crowns him with flowers and makes him all her joy:
    And now they never meet in grove or green,
    By fountain clear, or spangled starlight sheen,
    But they do square, that all their elves for fear   30
    Creep into acorn-cups and hide them there.

FAIRY
    Either I mistake your shape and making quite,

Or else you are that shrewd and knavish sprite
Called Robin Goodfellow: are not you he
That frights the maidens of the villagery; 35
Skim milk, and sometimes labour in the quern
And bootless make the breathless housewife churn;
And sometime make the drink to bear no barm;
Mislead night-wanderers, laughing at their harm?
Those that Hobgoblin call you, and sweet Puck, 40
You do their work, and they shall have good luck:
Are not you he?

PUCK   Thou speak'st aright;
I am that merry wanderer of the night.
I jest to Oberon and make him smile
When I a fat and bean-fed horse beguile, 45
Neighing in likeness of a filly foal:
And sometime lurk I in a gossip's bowl,
In very likeness of a roasted crab,
And when she drinks, against her lips I bob
And on her withered dewlap pour the ale. 50
The wisest aunt, telling the saddest tale,
Sometime for three-foot stool mistaketh me;
Then slip I from her bum, down topples she,
And "tailor" cries, and falls into a cough;
And then the whole quire hold their hips and laugh, 55
And waxen in their mirth and neeze and swear
A merrier hour was never wasted there.
But, room, fairy! Here comes Oberon.

FAIRY
And here my mistress. Would that he were gone!
Enter, from one side, Oberon, with his train; from the other, Titania, with hers.

OBERON
Ill met by moonlight, proud Titania. 60

TITANIA
What, jealous Oberon! Fairies, skip hence:
I have forsworn his bed and company.

OBERON
Tarry, rash wanton: am not I thy lord?

Notes

A "quern" is a hand grinder.

TITANIA

    Then I must be thy lady: but I know
    When thou hast stolen away from fairy land,   65
    And in the shape of Corin sat all day,
    Playing on pipes of corn and versing love
    To amorous Phillida. Why art thou here,
    Come from the farthest steep of India?
    But that, forsooth, the bouncing Amazon,   70
    Your buskined mistress and your warrior love,
    To Theseus must be wedded, and you come
    To give their bed joy and prosperity.

OBERON

    How canst thou thus, for shame, Titania,
    Glance at my credit with Hippolyta,   75
    Knowing I know thy love to Theseus?
    Didst thou not lead him through the glimmering night
    From Perigenia, whom he ravished?
    And make him with fair Aegles break his faith,
    With Ariadne and Antiopa?   80

TITANIA

    These are the forgeries of jealousy:
    And never, since the middle summer's spring,
    Met we on hill, in dale, forest or mead,
    By paved fountain or by rushy brook,
    Or in the beached margent of the sea,   85
    To dance our ringlets to the whistling wind,
    But with thy brawls thou hast disturbed our sport.
    Therefore the winds, piping to us in vain,
    As in revenge, have sucked up from the sea
    Contagious fogs; which falling in the land   90
    Hath every pelting river made so proud
    That they have overborne their continents:
    The ox hath therefore stretched his yoke in vain,
    The ploughman lost his sweat, and the green corn
    Hath rotted ere his youth attained a beard;   95
    The fold stands empty in the drowned field,
    And crows are fatted with the murrion flock;
    The nine-men's morris is filled up with mud,
    And the quaint mazes in the wanton green
    For lack of tread are undistinguishable: 100

Notes:

Names of Theseus' various love interests, according to Plutarch.

The human mortals want their winter cheer;
No night is now with hymn or carol blest:
Therefore the moon, the governess of floods,
Pale in her anger, washes all the air,
That rheumatic diseases do abound: 105
And thorough this distemperature we see
The seasons alter: hoary-headed frosts
Fall in the fresh lap of the crimson rose,
And on old Hiems' thin and icy crown
An odorous chaplet of sweet summer buds 110
Is, as in mockery, set: the spring, the summer,
The childing autumn, angry winter, change
Their wonted liveries, and the mazed world,
By their increase, now knows not which is which:
And this same progeny of evils comes 115
From our debate, from our dissension;
We are their parents and original.

OBERON
    Do you amend it then; it lies in you:
    Why should Titania cross her Oberon?
    I do but beg a little changeling boy, 120
    To be my henchman.

TITANIA   Set your heart at rest:
    The fairy land buys not the child of me.
    His mother was a votaress of my order:
    And, in the spiced Indian air, by night,
    Full often hath she gossiped by my side, 125
    And sat with me on Neptune's yellow sands,
    Marking the embarked traders on the flood,
    When we have laughed to see the sails conceive
    And grow big-bellied with the wanton wind;
    Which she, with pretty and with swimming gait 130
    Following,—her womb then rich with my young squire,—
    Would imitate, and sail upon the land,
    To fetch me trifles, and return again,
    As from a voyage, rich with merchandise.
    But she, being mortal, of that boy did die; 135
    And for her sake do I rear up her boy,
    And for her sake I will not part with him.

Notes

Hiems is the god of winter.

Notes

OBERON
   How long within this wood intend you stay?

TITANIA
   Perchance till after Theseus' wedding-day.
   If you will patiently dance in our round   140
   And see our moonlight revels, go with us;
   If not, shun me, and I will spare your haunts.

OBERON
   Give me that boy, and I will go with thee.

TITANIA
   Not for thy fairy kingdom. Fairies, away!
   We shall chide downright, if I longer stay.   145
      Exit Titania with her train.

OBERON
   Well, go thy way: thou shalt not from this grove
   Till I torment thee for this injury.
   My gentle Puck, come hither. Thou rememberest
   Since once I sat upon a promontory,
   And heard a mermaid on a dolphin's back   150
   Uttering such dulcet and harmonious breath
   That the rude sea grew civil at her song
   And certain stars shot madly from their spheres,
   To hear the sea-maid's music?

PUCK: I remember.

OBERON
   That very time I saw, but thou couldst not,   155
   Flying between the cold moon and the earth,
   Cupid all armed: a certain aim he took
   At a fair vestal throned by the west,
   And loosed his love-shaft smartly from his bow,
   As it should pierce a hundred thousand hearts;   160
   But I might see young Cupid's fiery shaft
   Quenched in the chaste beams of the watery moon,
   And the imperial votaress passed on,
   In maiden meditation, fancy-free.
   Yet marked I where the bolt of Cupid fell: 165
   It fell upon a little western flower,
   Before milk-white, now purple with love's wound,

  And maidens call it love-in-idleness.
  Fetch me that flower; the herb I shewed thee once:
  The juice of it on sleeping eye-lids laid   170
  Will make or man or woman madly dote
  Upon the next live creature that it sees.
  Fetch me this herb; and be thou here again
  Ere the leviathan can swim a league.

PUCK
  I'll put a girdle round about the earth   175
  In forty minutes.
   Exit Puck.

OBERON   Having once this juice,
  I'll watch Titania when she is asleep,
  And drop the liquor of it in her eyes.
  The next thing then she waking looks upon,
  Be it on lion, bear, or wolf, or bull,   180
  On meddling monkey, or on busy ape,
  She shall pursue it with the soul of love:
  And ere I take this charm from off her sight,
  As I can take it with another herb,
  I'll make her render up her page to me.   185
  But who comes here? I am invisible;
  And I will overhear their conference.
   Enter Demetrius, Helena following him.

DEMETRIUS
  I love thee not, therefore pursue me not.
  Where is Lysander and fair Hermia?
  The one I'll slay, the other slayeth me.   190
  Thou told'st me they were stolen unto this wood;
  And here am I, and wood within this wood,
  Because I cannot meet my Hermia.
  Hence, get thee gone, and follow me no more.

HELENA
  You draw me, you hard-hearted adamant;   195
  But yet you draw not iron, for my heart
  Is true as steel: leave you your power to draw,
  And I shall have no power to follow you.

Notes

Notes

DEMETRIUS
    Do I entice you? Do I speak you fair?
    Or, rather, do I not in plainest truth   200
    Tell you, I do not, nor I cannot love you?

HELENA
    And even for that do I love you the more.
    I am your spaniel; and, Demetrius,
    The more you beat me, I will fawn on you:
    Use me but as your spaniel, spurn me, strike me,   205
    Neglect me, lose me; only give me leave,
    Unworthy as I am, to follow you.
    What worser place can I beg in your love,—
    And yet a place of high respect with me,—
    Than to be used as you use your dog?   210

DEMETRIUS
    Tempt not too much the hatred of my spirit;
    For I am sick when I do look on thee.

HELENA
    And I am sick when I look not on you.

DEMETRIUS
    You do impeach your modesty too much,
    To leave the city and commit yourself   215
    Into the hands of one that loves you not;
    To trust the opportunity of night
    And the ill counsel of a desert place
    With the rich worth of your virginity.

HELENA
    Your virtue is my privilege: for that   220
    It is not night when I do see your face,
    Therefore I think I am not in the night;
    Nor doth this wood lack worlds of company,
    For you, in my respect, are all the world:
    Then how can it be said I am alone,   225
    When all the world is here to look on me?

DEMETRIUS
    I'll run from thee and hide me in the brakes,
    And leave thee to the mercy of wild beasts.

HELENA
    The wildest hath not such a heart as you.
    Run when you will, the story shall be changed: 230
    Apollo flies, and Daphne holds the chase;
    The dove pursues the griffin; the mild hind
    Makes speed to catch the tiger; bootless speed,
    When cowardice pursues and valour flies.

DEMETRIUS
    I will not stay thy questions; let me go: 235
    Or, if thou follow me, do not believe
    But I shall do thee mischief in the wood.

HELENA
    Ay, in the temple, in the town, the field,
    You do me mischief. Fie, Demetrius!
    Your wrongs do set a scandal on my sex: 240
    We cannot fight for love, as men may do;
    We should be wooed and were not made to woo.
        Exit Demetrius.
    I'll follow thee and make a heaven of hell,
    To die upon the hand I love so well.
        Exit Helena.

OBERON
    Fare thee well, nymph: ere he do leave this grove,   245
    Thou shalt fly him and he shall seek thy love.
        Re-enter Puck.
    Hast thou the flower there? Welcome, wanderer.

PUCK
    Ay, there it is.

OBERON   I pray thee, give it me.
    I know a bank where the wild thyme blows,
    Where oxlips and the nodding violet grows,   250
    Quite over-canopied with luscious woodbine,
    With sweet musk-roses and with eglantine:
    There sleeps Titania sometime of the night,
    Lulled in these flowers with dances and delight;
    And there the snake throws her enamelled skin,   255
    Weed wide enough to wrap a fairy in:
    And with the juice of this I'll streak her eyes,

Notes

And make her full of hateful fantasies.
Take thou some of it, and seek through this grove:
A sweet Athenian lady is in love   260
With a disdainful youth: anoint his eyes;
But do it when the next thing he espies
May be the lady: thou shalt know the man
By the Athenian garments he hath on.
Effect it with some care, that he may prove   265
More fond on her than she upon her love:
And look thou meet me ere the first cock crow.

PUCK
  Fear not, my lord, your servant shall do so.
    Exeunt.

Act II, Scene 2

Setting: Another part of the wood.
Enter Titania, with her train.

TITANIA
    Come, now a roundel and a fairy song;
    Then, for the third part of a minute, hence;
    Some to kill cankers in the musk-rose buds,
    Some war with rere-mice for their leathern wings,
    To make my small elves coats, and some keep back 5
    The clamorous owl that nightly hoots and wonders
    At our quaint spirits. Sing me now asleep;
    Then to your offices and let me rest.
      [The Fairies sing.]

FIRST FAIRY
    You spotted snakes with double tongue,
      Thorny hedgehogs, be not seen; 10
    Newts and blind-worms, do no wrong,
      Come not near our fairy queen.

FAIRY CHORUS
    Philomel, with melody
    Sing in our sweet lullaby;
    Lulla, lulla, lullaby, lulla, lulla, lullaby: 15
      Never harm,
      Nor spell nor charm,
    Come our lovely lady nigh;
    So, good night, with lullaby.

FIRST FAIRY
    Weaving spiders, come not here; 20
      Hence, you long-legged spinners, hence!
    Beetles black, approach not near;
      Worm nor snail, do no offence.

FAIRY CHORUS
    Philomel, with melody, etc.
  Titania sleeps.

SECOND FAIRY
    Hence, away! Now all is well: 25
    One aloof stand sentinel.
  Exeunt Fairies.

Notes

"Rere-mice" are bats.

Notes

Enter Oberon and squeezes the flower on Titania's eyelids.

OBERON
    What thou seest when thou dost wake,
    Do it for thy true-love take,
    Love and languish for his sake:
    Be it ounce, or cat, or bear,   30
    Pard, or boar with bristled hair,
    In thy eye that shall appear
    When thou wakest, it is thy dear:
    Wake when some vile thing is near.

Exit Oberon.
Enter Lysander and Hermia.

An "ounce" is a lynx, and a "pard" is a leopard.

LYSANDER
    Fair love, you faint with wandering in the wood;   35
    And to speak troth, I have forgot our way:
    We'll rest us, Hermia, if you think it good,
    And tarry for the comfort of the day.

HERMIA
    Be it so, Lysander: find you out a bed;
    For I upon this bank will rest my head.   40

LYSANDER
    One turf shall serve as pillow for us both;
    One heart, one bed, two bosoms and one troth.

HERMIA
    Nay, good Lysander; for my sake, my dear,
    Lie further off yet, do not lie so near.

LYSANDER
    O, take the sense, sweet, of my innocence!   45
    Love takes the meaning in love's conference.
    I mean, that my heart unto yours is knit
    So that but one heart we can make of it;
    Two bosoms interchained with an oath;
    So then two bosoms and a single troth.   50
    Then by your side no bed-room me deny;
    For lying so, Hermia, I do not lie.

HERMIA
    Lysander riddles very prettily:

Now much beshrew my manners and my pride,
If Hermia meant to say Lysander lied. 55
But, gentle friend, for love and courtesy
Lie further off; in human modesty,
Such separation as may well be said
Becomes a virtuous bachelor and a maid,
So far be distant; and, good night, sweet friend: 60
Thy love ne'er alter till thy sweet life end!

LYSANDER
Amen, amen, to that fair prayer, say I;
And then end life when I end loyalty!
Here is my bed: sleep give thee all his rest!

HERMIA
With half that wish the wisher's eyes be press'd! 65
[They sleep.]
Enter Puck.

PUCK
    Through the forest have I gone.
    But Athenian found I none,
    On whose eyes I might approve
    This flower's force in stirring love.
    Night and silence.—Who is here? 70
    Weeds of Athens he doth wear:
    This is he, my master said,
    Despised the Athenian maid;
    And here the maiden, sleeping sound,
    On the dank and dirty ground. 75
    Pretty soul! she durst not lie
    Near this lack-love, this kill-courtesy.
    Churl, upon thy eyes I throw
    All the power this charm doth owe.
    [He squeezes the flower onto Lysander's eyelids.]
    When thou wakest, let love forbid 80
    Sleep his seat on thy eyelid:
    So awake when I am gone;
    For I must now to Oberon.
Exit Puck.
Enter Demetrius and Helena, running.

Notes

HELENA
    Stay, though thou kill me, sweet Demetrius.

DEMETRIUS
    I charge thee, hence, and do not haunt me thus.   85

HELENA
    O, wilt thou darkling leave me? Do not so.

DEMETRIUS
    Stay, on thy peril: I alone will go.
        Exit Demetrius.

HELENA
    O, I am out of breath in this fond chase!
    The more my prayer, the lesser is my grace.
    Happy is Hermia, wheresoe'er she lies;   90
    For she hath blessed and attractive eyes.
    How came her eyes so bright? Not with salt tears:
    If so, my eyes are oftener washed than hers.
    No, no, I am as ugly as a bear;
    For beasts that meet me run away for fear: 95
    Therefore no marvel though Demetrius
    Do, as a monster, fly my presence thus.
    What wicked and dissembling glass of mine
    Made me compare with Hermia's sphery eyne?
    But who is here? Lysander! on the ground!   100
    Dead? or asleep? I see no blood, no wound.
    Lysander, if you live, good sir, awake.

LYSANDER *[Awaking.]*
    And run through fire I will for thy sweet sake.
    Transparent Helena! Nature shows art,
    That through thy bosom makes me see thy heart.   105
    Where is Demetrius? O, how fit a word
    Is that vile name to perish on my sword!

HELENA
    Do not say so, Lysander; say not so;
    What though he love your Hermia? Lord, what though?
    Yet Hermia still loves you: then be content.   110

LYSANDER
    Content with Hermia! No; I do repent

The tedious minutes I with her have spent.
Not Hermia, but Helena I love:
Who will not change a raven for a dove?
The will of man is by his reason swayed; 115
And reason says you are the worthier maid.
Things growing are not ripe until their season:
So I, being young, till now ripe not to reason;
And touching now the point of human skill,
Reason becomes the marshal to my will 120
And leads me to your eyes, where I o'erlook
Love's stories written in love's richest book.

HELENA

Wherefore was I to this keen mockery born?
When at your hands did I deserve this scorn?
Is't not enough, is't not enough, young man, 125
That I did never, no, nor never can,
Deserve a sweet look from Demetrius' eye,
But you must flout my insufficiency?
Good troth, you do me wrong; good sooth, you do,
In such disdainful manner me to woo. 130
But fare you well: perforce I must confess
I thought you lord of more true gentleness.
O, that a lady, of one man refused,
Should of another therefore be abused!

Exit Helena.

LYSANDER

She sees not Hermia. Hermia, sleep thou there: 135
And never mayst thou come Lysander near!
For as a surfeit of the sweetest things
The deepest loathing to the stomach brings,
Or as the heresies that men do leave
Are hated most of those they did deceive, 140
So thou, my surfeit and my heresy,
Of all be hated, but the most of me!
And, all my powers, address your love and might
To honour Helen and to be her knight!

Exit Lysander.

HERMIA *[Awaking.]*

Help me, Lysander, help me! Do thy best 145

Notes

Notes

To pluck this crawling serpent from my breast!
Ay me, for pity! What a dream was here!
Lysander, look how I do quake with fear:
Methought a serpent eat my heart away,
And you sat smiling at his cruel prey.   150
Lysander! What, removed? Lysander! lord!
What, out of hearing? gone? No sound, no word?
Alack, where are you? Speak, an if you hear;
Speak, of all loves! I swoon almost with fear.
No? then I well perceive you are not nigh.   155
Either death or you I'll find immediately.

Exit Hermia.

Act III, Scene 1

Setting: The wood. Titania lying asleep.
Enter Quince, Snug, Bottom, Flute, Snout, and Starveling.

BOTTOM: Are we all met?

QUINCE: Pat, pat; and here's a marvellous convenient place for our rehearsal. This green plot shall be our stage, this hawthorn-brake our tiring-house; and we will do it in action as we will do it before the duke.

BOTTOM: Peter Quince,—

QUINCE: What sayest thou, bully Bottom?

BOTTOM: There are things in this comedy of Pyramus and Thisby that will never please. First, Pyramus must draw a sword to kill himself; which the ladies cannot abide. How answer you that?

SNOUT: By'r lakin, a parlous fear.

STARVELING: I believe we must leave the killing out, when all is done.

BOTTOM: Not a whit: I have a device to make all well. Write me a prologue; and let the prologue seem to say, we will do no harm with our swords, and that Pyramus is not killed indeed; and, for the more better assurance, tell them that I, Pyramus, am not Pyramus, but Bottom the weaver: this will put them out of fear.

QUINCE: Well, we will have such a prologue; and it shall be written in eight and six.

BOTTOM: No, make it two more; let it be written in eight and eight.

SNOUT: Will not the ladies be afeard of the lion?

STARVELING: I fear it, I promise you.

BOTTOM: Masters, you ought to consider with yourselves: to bring in—God shield us!—a lion among ladies is a most dreadful thing; for there is not a more fearful wild-fowl than your lion living; and we ought to look to't.

Notes

SNOUT: Therefore another prologue must tell he is not a lion.

BOTTOM: Nay, you must name his name, and half his face must be seen through the lion's neck: and he himself must speak through, saying thus, or to the same defect,—"Ladies,"—or "Fair-ladies—I would wish you,"—or "I would request you,"—or "I would entreat you,—not to fear, not to tremble: my life for yours. If you think I come hither as a lion, it were pity of my life: no I am no such thing; I am a man as other men are"; and there indeed let him name his name, and tell them plainly he is Snug the joiner.

QUINCE: Well, it shall be so. But there is two hard things; that is, to bring the moonlight into a chamber; for, you know, Pyramus and Thisby meet by moonlight.

SNOUT : Doth the moon shine that night we play our play?

BOTTOM: A calendar, a calendar! Look in the almanac; find out moonshine, find out moonshine.

QUINCE: Yes, it doth shine that night.

BOTTOM: Why, then may you leave a casement of the great chamber window, where we play, open, and the moon may shine in at the casement.

QUINCE: Ay; or else one must come in with a bush of thorns and a lanthorn, and say he comes to disfigure, or to present, the person of Moonshine. Then, there is another thing: we must have a wall in the great chamber; for Pyramus and Thisby, says the story, did talk through the chink of a wall.

SNOUT: You can never bring in a wall. What say you, Bottom?

BOTTOM: Some man or other must present Wall: and let him have some plaster, or some loam, or some rough-cast about him, to signify wall; and let him hold his fingers thus, and through that cranny shall Pyramus and Thisby whisper.

QUINCE: If that may be, then all is well. Come, sit down, every mother's son, and rehearse your parts. Pyramus, you begin: when you have spoken your speech, enter into that brake: and so every one according to his cue.
Enter Puck behind.

PUCK
What hempen home-spuns have we swaggering here,
So near the cradle of the fairy queen?
What, a play toward! I'll be an auditor;
An actor too, perhaps, if I see cause.

QUINCE: Speak, Pyramus. Thisby, stand forth.

BOTTOM *[As Pyramus]*
Thisby, the flowers of odious savours sweet,—

QUINCE: Odorous, odorous.

BOTTOM *[As Pyramus]*
—odours savours sweet:
    So hath thy breath, my dearest Thisby dear.
But hark, a voice! Stay thou but here awhile,
    And by and by I will to thee appear.
Exit Bottom.

PUCK
A stranger Pyramus than e'er played here.
Exit Puck.

FLUTE: Must I speak now?

QUINCE: Ay, marry, must you; for you must understand he goes but to see a noise that he heard, and is to come again.

FLUTE *[As Thisby]*
Most radiant Pyramus, most lily-white of hue,
    Of colour like the red rose on triumphant brier,
Most bristly juvenal and eke most lovely Jew,
    As true as truest horse that yet would never tire,
I'll meet thee, Pyramus, at Ninny's tomb.

QUINCE: "Ninus' tomb," man: why, you must not speak that yet; that you answer to Pyramus: you speak all

your part at once, cues and all. Pyramus, enter: your
cue is past; it is, "never tire." 95

FLUTE: O,
   [As Thisby]
   —As true as truest horse, that yet would never tire.
      Re-enter Puck, and Bottom with an ass' head.

BOTTOM *[As Pyramus]*
   If I were fair, Thisby, I were only thine.

QUINCE: O monstrous! O strange! We are haunted. Pray, 100
   masters! Fly, masters! Help!
      Exeunt Quince, Snug, Flute, Snout, and Starveling.

PUCK
   I'll follow you, I'll lead you about a round,
      Through bog, through bush, through brake, through brier:
   Sometime a horse I'll be, sometime a hound,
      A hog, a headless bear, sometime a fire; 105
   And neigh, and bark, and grunt, and roar, and burn,
   Like horse, hound, hog, bear, fire, at every turn.
      Exit Puck.

BOTTOM: Why do they run away? This is a knavery of them
   to make me afeard.
      Re-enter Snout.

SNOUT: O Bottom, thou art changed! What do I see 110
   on thee?

BOTTOM: What do you see? You see an ass-head of your
   own, do you?
      Exit Snout. Re-enter Quince.

QUINCE: Bless thee, Bottom! Bless thee! Thou art
   translated. 115
      Exit Quince.

BOTTOM: I see their knavery: this is to make an ass of
   me; to fright me, if they could. But I will not stir from
   this place, do what they can: I will walk up and down
   here, and I will sing, that they shall hear I am not afraid.
   [Sings.]
      The ousel cock so black of hue, 120

> With orange-tawny bill,
> The throstle with his note so true,
> The wren with little quill,—

TITANIA *[Awaking.]*
> What angel wakes me from my flowery bed?

BOTTOM *[Sings.]*
> The finch, the sparrow and the lark, 125
> The plain-song cuckoo gray,
> Whose note full many a man doth mark,
> And dares not answer nay;—
> for, indeed, who would set his wit to so foolish a bird?
> Who would give a bird the lie, though he cry "cuckoo" 130
> never so?

TITANIA
> I pray thee, gentle mortal, sing again:
> Mine ear is much enamoured of thy note;
> So is mine eye enthralled to thy shape;
> And thy fair virtue's force perforce doth move me 135
> On the first view to say, to swear, I love thee.

BOTTOM: Methinks, mistress, you should have little reason for that: and yet, to say the truth, reason and love keep little company together now-a-days; the more the pity that some honest neighbours will not make them 140 friends. Nay, I can gleek upon occasion.

TITANIA
> Thou art as wise as thou art beautiful.

BOTTOM: Not so, neither: but if I had wit enough to get out of this wood, I have enough to serve mine own turn. 145

TITANIA
> Out of this wood do not desire to go:
> Thou shalt remain here, whether thou wilt or no.
> I am a spirit of no common rate;
> The summer still doth tend upon my state;
> And I do love thee: therefore, go with me; 150
> I'll give thee fairies to attend on thee,
> And they shall fetch thee jewels from the deep,
> And sing while thou on pressed flowers dost sleep;

Notes

To "gleek" is to wisecrack.

    And I will purge thy mortal grossness so
    That thou shalt like an airy spirit go.   155
    Peaseblossom! Cobweb! Moth! and Mustardseed!

Enter fairies Peaseblossom, Cobweb, Moth, and Mustardseed.

PEASEBLOSSOM: Ready.

COBWEB: And I.

MOTH: And I.

MUSTARDSEED: And I.

ALL: Where shall we go?

TITANIA
    Be kind and courteous to this gentleman;
    Hop in his walks and gambol in his eyes;   160
    Feed him with apricocks and dewberries,
    With purple grapes, green figs, and mulberries;
    The honey-bags steal from the humble-bees,
    And for night-tapers crop their waxen thighs
    And light them at the fiery glow-worm's eyes,   165
    To have my love to bed and to arise;
    And pluck the wings from painted butterflies
    To fan the moonbeams from his sleeping eyes:
    Nod to him, elves, and do him courtesies.

PEASEBLOSSOM: Hail, mortal!   170

COBWEB: Hail!

MOTH: Hail!

MUSTARDSEED: Hail!

BOTTOM: I cry your worship's mercy, heartily: I beseech
    your worship's name.   175

COBWEB: Cobweb.

BOTTOM: I shall desire you of more acquaintance, good
    Master Cobweb: if I cut my finger, I shall make bold with
    you. Your name, honest gentleman?

PEASEBLOSSOM: Peaseblossom.   180

BOTTOM: I pray you, commend me to Mistress Squash,

your mother, and to Master Peascod, your father. Good Master Peaseblossom, I shall desire you of more acquaintance too. Your name, I beseech you, sir?

MUSTARDSEED: Mustardseed. 185

BOTTOM: Good Master Mustardseed, I know your patience well: that same cowardly, giant-like ox-beef hath devoured many a gentleman of your house: I promise you your kindred hath made my eyes water ere now. I desire you of more acquaintance, good Master 190 Mustardseed.

TITANIA
Come, wait upon him; lead him to my bower.
    The moon, methinks, looks with a watery eye;
And when she weeps, weeps every little flower,
    Lamenting some enforced chastity. 195
    Tie up my love's tongue, bring him silently.
Exeunt.

Notes

Act III, Scene 2
Setting: Another part of the wood.
Enter Oberon.

OBERON
    I wonder if Titania be awaked;
    Then, what it was that next came in her eye,
    Which she must dote on in extremity.
        Enter Puck.
    Here comes my messenger. How now, mad spirit!
    What night-rule now about this haunted grove?   5

PUCK
    My mistress with a monster is in love.
    Near to her close and consecrated bower,
    While she was in her dull and sleeping hour,
    A crew of patches, rude mechanicals,
    That work for bread upon Athenian stalls,   10
    Were met together to rehearse a play
    Intended for great Theseus' nuptial-day.
    The shallowest thick-skin of that barren sort,
    Who Pyramus presented, in their sport
    Forsook his scene and entered in a brake   15
    When I did him at this advantage take,
    An ass' nole I fixed on his head:
    Anon his Thisby must be answered,
    And forth my mimic comes. When they him spy,
    As wild geese that the creeping fowler eye,   20
    Or russet-pated choughs, many in sort,
    Rising and cawing at the gun's report,
    Sever themselves and madly sweep the sky,
    So, at his sight, away his fellows fly;
    And, at our stamp, here o'er and o'er one falls;   25
    He "murder" cries and help from Athens calls.
    Their sense thus weak, lost with their fears thus strong,
    Made senseless things begin to do them wrong;
    For briers and thorns at their apparel snatch;
    Some sleeves, some hats, from yielders all things catch.   30
    I led them on in this distracted fear,
    And left sweet Pyramus translated there:
    When in that moment, so it came to pass,
    Titania waked and straightway loved an ass.

OBERON
> This falls out better than I could devise. 35
> But hast thou yet latched the Athenian's eyes
> With the love-juice, as I did bid thee do?

PUCK
> I took him sleeping,—that is finished too,—
> And the Athenian woman by his side:
> That, when he waked, of force she must be eyed. 40

Enter Hermia and Demetrius.

OBERON
> Stand close: this is the same Athenian.

PUCK
> This is the woman, but not this the man.

DEMETRIUS
> O, why rebuke you him that loves you so?
> Lay breath so bitter on your bitter foe.

HERMIA
> Now I but chide; but I should use thee worse, 45
> For thou, I fear, hast given me cause to curse,
> If thou hast slain Lysander in his sleep,
> Being o'er shoes in blood, plunge in the deep,
> And kill me too.
> The sun was not so true unto the day 50
> As he to me: would he have stolen away
> From sleeping Hermia? I'll believe as soon
> This whole earth may be bored and that the moon
> May through the centre creep and so displease
> Her brother's noontide with Antipodes. 55
> It cannot be but thou hast murdered him;
> So should a murderer look, so dead, so grim.

DEMETRIUS
> So should the murdered look, and so should I,
> Pierced through the heart with your stern cruelty:
> Yet you, the murderer, look as bright, as clear, 60
> As yonder Venus in her glimmering sphere.

HERMIA
> What's this to my Lysander? Where is he?

Ah, good Demetrius, wilt thou give him me?

DEMETRIUS
I had rather give his carcass to my hounds.

HERMIA
Out, dog! out, cur! Thou drivest me past the bounds 65
Of maiden's patience. Hast thou slain him, then?
Henceforth be never numbered among men!
O, once tell true, tell true, even for my sake!
Durst thou have looked upon him being awake,
And hast thou killed him sleeping? O brave touch! 70
Could not a worm, an adder, do so much?
An adder did it; for with doubler tongue
Than thine, thou serpent, never adder stung.

DEMETRIUS
You spend your passion on a misprised mood:
I am not guilty of Lysander's blood; 75
Nor is he dead, for aught that I can tell.

HERMIA
I pray thee, tell me then that he is well.

DEMETRIUS
An if I could, what should I get therefore?

HERMIA
A privilege never to see me more.
And from thy hated presence part I so: 80
See me no more, whether he be dead or no.
Exit Hermia.

DEMETRIUS
There is no following her in this fierce vein:
Here therefore for a while I will remain.
So sorrow's heaviness doth heavier grow
For debt that bankrupt sleep doth sorrow owe: 85
Which now in some slight measure it will pay,
If for his tender here I make some stay.
[Lies down and sleeps.]

OBERON
What hast thou done? thou hast mistaken quite
And laid the love-juice on some true-love's sight:

                Of thy misprision must perforce ensue   90
                Some true love turned and not a false turned true.

PUCK
                Then fate o'er-rules, that, one man holding troth,
                A million fail, confounding oath on oath.

OBERON
                About the wood go swifter than the wind,
                And Helena of Athens look thou find: 95
                All fancy-sick she is and pale of cheer,
                With sighs of love, that costs the fresh blood dear:
                By some illusion see thou bring her here:
                I'll charm his eyes against she do appear.

PUCK
                I go, I go; look how I go,   100
                Swifter than arrow from the Tartar's bow.
            Exit Puck.

OBERON
                Flower of this purple dye,
                Hit with Cupid's archery,
                Sink in apple of his eye.
                [He squeezes the flower onto Demetrius' eyelids.]
                When his love he doth espy,   105
                Let her shine as gloriously
                As the Venus of the sky.
                When thou wakest, if she be by,
                Beg of her for remedy.
            Re-enter Puck.

PUCK
                Captain of our fairy band,   110
                Helena is here at hand;
                And the youth, mistook by me,
                Pleading for a lover's fee.
                Shall we their fond pageant see?
                Lord, what fools these mortals be!   115

OBERON
                Stand aside: the noise they make
                Will cause Demetrius to awake.

Notes

PUCK
    Then will two at once woo one;
    That must needs be sport alone;
    And those things do best please me   120
    That befall preposterously.
Enter Lysander and Helena.

LYSANDER
  Why should you think that I should woo in scorn?
    Scorn and derision never come in tears:
  Look, when I vow, I weep; and vows so born,
    In their nativity all truth appears.   125
  How can these things in me seem scorn to you,
  Bearing the badge of faith to prove them true?

HELENA
  You do advance your cunning more and more.
    When truth kills truth, O devilish-holy fray!
  These vows are Hermia's: will you give her o'er?   130
    Weigh oath with oath, and you will nothing weigh:
  Your vows to her and me, put in two scales,
  Will even weigh, and both as light as tales.

LYSANDER
  I had no judgment when to her I swore.

HELENA
  Nor none, in my mind, now you give her o'er.   135

LYSANDER
  Demetrius loves her, and he loves not you.

DEMETRIUS *[Awaking]*
  O Helena, goddess, nymph, perfect, divine!
  To what, my love, shall I compare thine eyne?
  Crystal is muddy. O, how ripe in show
  Thy lips, those kissing cherries, tempting grow!   140
  That pure congealed white, high Taurus snow,
  Fanned with the eastern wind, turns to a crow
  When thou hold'st up thy hand: O, let me kiss
  This princess of pure white, this seal of bliss!

HELENA
  O spite! O hell! I see you all are bent   145

To set against me for your merriment:
If you were civil and knew courtesy,
You would not do me thus much injury.
Can you not hate me, as I know you do,
But you must join in souls to mock me too? 150
If you were men, as men you are in show,
You would not use a gentle lady so;
To vow, and swear, and superpraise my parts,
When I am sure you hate me with your hearts.
You both are rivals, and love Hermia; 155
And now both rivals, to mock Helena:
A trim exploit, a manly enterprise,
To conjure tears up in a poor maid's eyes
With your derision! None of noble sort
Would so offend a virgin, and extort 160
A poor soul's patience, all to make you sport.

LYSANDER
You are unkind, Demetrius; be not so;
For you love Hermia; this you know I know:
And here, with all good will, with all my heart,
In Hermia's love I yield you up my part; 165
And yours of Helena to me bequeath,
Whom I do love and will do till my death.

HELENA
Never did mockers waste more idle breath.

DEMETRIUS
Lysander, keep thy Hermia; I will none:
If e'er I loved her, all that love is gone. 170
My heart to her but as guest-wise sojourned,
And now to Helen is it home returned,
There to remain.

LYSANDER   Helen, it is not so.

DEMETRIUS
Disparage not the faith thou dost not know,
Lest, to thy peril, thou aby it dear. 175
Look where thy love comes; yonder is thy dear.
Re-enter Hermia.

Notes

Notes

HERMIA
   Dark night, that from the eye his function takes,
   The ear more quick of apprehension makes;
   Wherein it doth impair the seeing sense,
   It pays the hearing double recompense.   180
   Thou art not by mine eye, Lysander, found;
   Mine ear, I thank it, brought me to thy sound.
   But why unkindly didst thou leave me so?

LYSANDER
   Why should he stay, whom love doth press to go?

HERMIA
   What love could press Lysander from my side?   185

LYSANDER
   Lysander's love, that would not let him bide,
   Fair Helena, who more engilds the night
   Than all yon fiery oes and eyes of light.
   Why seek'st thou me? Could not this make thee know,
   The hate I bear thee made me leave thee so?   190

HERMIA
   You speak not as you think: it cannot be.

HELENA
   Lo, she is one of this confederacy!
   Now I perceive they have conjoined all three
   To fashion this false sport, in spite of me.
   Injurious Hermia! most ungrateful maid!   195
   Have you conspired, have you with these contrived
   To bait me with this foul derision?
   Is all the counsel that we two have shared,
   The sisters' vows, the hours that we have spent,
   When we have chid the hasty-footed time   200
   For parting us,—O, is all forgot?
   All school-days' friendship, childhood innocence?
   We, Hermia, like two artificial gods,
   Have with our needles created both one flower,
   Both on one sampler, sitting on one cushion,   205
   Both warbling of one song, both in one key,
   As if our hands, our sides, voices and minds
   Had been incorporate. So we grew together,
   Like to a double cherry, seeming parted,

But yet an union in partition; 210
Two lovely berries moulded on one stem;
So, with two seeming bodies, but one heart;
Two of the first, like coats in heraldry,
Due but to one and crowned with one crest.
And will you rent our ancient love asunder, 215
To join with men in scorning your poor friend?
It is not friendly, 'tis not maidenly:
Our sex, as well as I, may chide you for it,
Though I alone do feel the injury.

HERMIA
I am amazed at your passionate words. 220
I scorn you not: it seems that you scorn me.

HELENA
Have you not set Lysander, as in scorn,
To follow me and praise my eyes and face?
And made your other love, Demetrius,
Who even but now did spurn me with his foot, 225
To call me goddess, nymph, divine and rare,
Precious, celestial? Wherefore speaks he this
To her he hates? And wherefore doth Lysander
Deny your love, so rich within his soul,
And tender me, forsooth, affection, 230
But by your setting on, by your consent?
What though I be not so in grace as you,
So hung upon with love, so fortunate,
But miserable most, to love unloved?
This you should pity rather than despise. 235

HERMIA
I understand not what you mean by this.

HELENA
Ay, do, persever, counterfeit sad looks,
Make mouths upon me when I turn my back;
Wink each at other; hold the sweet jest up:
This sport, well carried, shall be chronicled. 240
If you have any pity, grace, or manners,
You would not make me such an argument.
But fare ye well: 'tis partly my own fault;
Which death or absence soon shall remedy.

Notes

Notes

LYSANDER
   Stay, gentle Helena; hear my excuse: 245
   My love, my life, my soul, fair Helena!

HELENA
   O excellent!

HERMIA   Sweet, do not scorn her so.

DEMETRIUS
   If she cannot entreat, I can compel.

LYSANDER
   Thou canst compel no more than she entreat:
   Thy threats have no more strength than her weak prayers.   250
   Helen, I love thee; by my life, I do:
   I swear by that which I will lose for thee,
   To prove him false that says I love thee not.

DEMETRIUS
   I say I love thee more than he can do.

LYSANDER
   If thou say so, withdraw, and prove it too.   255

DEMETRIUS
   Quick, come!

HERMIA   Lysander, whereto tends all this?

LYSANDER
   Away, you Ethiope!

DEMETRIUS   No, no; sir, yield.
   Seem to break loose; take on as you would follow,
   But yet come not: you are a tame man, go!

LYSANDER *[To Hermia.]*
   Hang off, thou cat, thou burr! Vile thing, let loose,   260
   Or I will shake thee from me like a serpent!

HERMIA
   Why are you grown so rude? What change is this?
   Sweet love,—

LYSANDER   Thy love! Out, tawny Tartar, out!
   Out, loathed medicine! O hated potion, hence!

HERMIA
  Do you not jest?

HELENA   Yes, sooth; and so do you.   265

LYSANDER
  Demetrius, I will keep my word with thee.

DEMETRIUS
  I would I had your bond, for I perceive
  A weak bond holds you: I'll not trust your word.

LYSANDER
  What, should I hurt her, strike her, kill her dead?
  Although I hate her, I'll not harm her so.   270

HERMIA
  What, can you do me greater harm than hate?
  Hate me! Wherefore? O me! What news, my love!
  Am not I Hermia? Are not you Lysander?
  I am as fair now as I was erewhile.
  Since night you loved me; yet since night you left me: 275
  Why, then you left me—O, the gods forbid!—
  In earnest, shall I say?

LYSANDER   Ay, by my life;
  And never did desire to see thee more.
  Therefore be out of hope, of question, of doubt;
  Be certain, nothing truer; 'tis no jest   280
  That I do hate thee and love Helena.

HERMIA *[To Helena.]*
  O me! You juggler! You canker-blossom!
  You thief of love! What, have you come by night
  And stolen my love's heart from him?

HELENA   Fine, i'faith!
  Have you no modesty, no maiden shame,   285
  No touch of bashfulness? What, will you tear
  Impatient answers from my gentle tongue?
  Fie, fie! You counterfeit, you puppet, you!

HERMIA
  Puppet? Why so? Ay, that way goes the game.
  Now I perceive that she hath made compare   290

Notes

    Between our statures; she hath urged her height;
    And with her personage, her tall personage,
    Her height, forsooth, she hath prevailed with him.
    And are you grown so high in his esteem
    Because I am so dwarfish and so low?   295
    How low am I, thou painted maypole? Speak;
    How low am I? I am not yet so low
    But that my nails can reach unto thine eyes.

HELENA
    I pray you, though you mock me, gentlemen,
    Let her not hurt me: I was never curst;   300
    I have no gift at all in shrewishness;
    I am a right maid for my cowardice:
    Let her not strike me. You perhaps may think,
    Because she is something lower than myself,
    That I can match her.

HERMIA   Lower! hark, again.   305

HELENA
    Good Hermia, do not be so bitter with me.
    I evermore did love you, Hermia,
    Did ever keep your counsels, never wronged you;
    Save that, in love unto Demetrius,
    I told him of your stealth unto this wood.   310
    He followed you; for love I followed him;
    But he hath chid me hence and threatened me
    To strike me, spurn me, nay, to kill me too:
    And now, so you will let me quiet go,
    To Athens will I bear my folly back   315
    And follow you no further: let me go:
    You see how simple and how fond I am.

HERMIA
    Why, get you gone: who is't that hinders you?

HELENA
    A foolish heart, that I leave here behind.

HERMIA
    What, with Lysander?

HELENA   With Demetrius.   320

LYSANDER
  Be not afraid; she shall not harm thee, Helena.

DEMETRIUS
  No, sir, she shall not, though you take her part.

HELENA
  O, when she's angry, she is keen and shrewd!
  She was a vixen when she went to school;
  And though she be but little, she is fierce. 325

HERMIA
  "Little" again! Nothing but "low" and "little"!
  Why will you suffer her to flout me thus?
  Let me come to her.

LYSANDER   Get you gone, you dwarf;
  You minimus, of hindering knot-grass made;
  You bead, you acorn.

DEMETRIUS   You are too officious 330
  In her behalf that scorns your services.
  Let her alone: speak not of Helena;
  Take not her part; for, if thou dost intend
  Never so little show of love to her,
  Thou shalt aby it.

LYSANDER   Now she holds me not; 335
  Now follow, if thou darest, to try whose right,
  Of thine or mine, is most in Helena.

DEMETRIUS
  Follow! Nay, I'll go with thee, cheek by jowl.
    Exeunt Lysander and Demetrius.

HERMIA
  You, mistress, all this coil is long of you:
  Nay, go not back.

HELENA   I will not trust you, I, 340
  Nor longer stay in your curst company.
  Your hands than mine are quicker for a fray,
  My legs are longer though, to run away.

HERMIA
  I am amazed, and know not what to say.

Exit Helena and Hermia.

OBERON
    This is thy negligence: still thou mistakest,   345
    Or else committest thy knaveries wilfully.

PUCK
    Believe me, king of shadows, I mistook.
    Did not you tell me I should know the man
    By the Athenian garment he had on?
    And so far blameless proves my enterprise,   350
    That I have 'nointed an Athenian's eyes;
    And so far am I glad it so did sort
    As this their jangling I esteem a sport.

OBERON
    Thou seest these lovers seek a place to fight:
    Hie therefore, Robin, overcast the night;   355
    The starry welkin cover thou anon
    With drooping fog as black as Acheron,
    And lead these testy rivals so astray
    As one come not within another's way.
    Like to Lysander sometime frame thy tongue,   360
    Then stir Demetrius up with bitter wrong;
    And sometime rail thou like Demetrius;
    And from each other look thou lead them thus,
    Till o'er their brows death-counterfeiting sleep
    With leaden legs and batty wings doth creep: 365
    Then crush this herb into Lysander's eye;
    Whose liquor hath this virtuous property,
    To take from thence all error with his might,
    And make his eyeballs roll with wonted sight.
    When they next wake, all this derision   370
    Shall seem a dream and fruitless vision,
    And back to Athens shall the lovers wend,
    With league whose date till death shall never end.
    Whiles I in this affair do thee employ,
    I'll to my queen and beg her Indian boy;   375
    And then I will her charmed eye release
    From monster's view, and all things shall be peace.

PUCK
    My fairy lord, this must be done with haste,

For night's swift dragons cut the clouds full fast,
And yonder shines Aurora's harbinger; 380
At whose approach, ghosts, wandering here and there,
Troop home to churchyards: damned spirits all,
That in crossways and floods have burial,
Already to their wormy beds are gone;
For fear lest day should look their shames upon, 385
They wilfully themselves exile from light
And must for aye consort with black-browed night.

OBERON

But we are spirits of another sort:
I with the morning's love have oft made sport,
And, like a forester, the groves may tread, 390
Even till the eastern gate, all fiery-red,
Opening on Neptune with fair blessed beams,
Turns into yellow gold his salt green streams.
But, notwithstanding, haste; make no delay:
We may effect this business yet ere day. 395

Exit Oberon.

PUCK

    Up and down, up and down,
    I will lead them up and down:
    I am feared in field and town:
    Goblin, lead them up and down.
Here comes one. 400

Re-enter Lysander.

LYSANDER

Where art thou, proud Demetrius? Speak thou now.

PUCK

Here, villain; drawn and ready. Where art thou?

LYSANDER

I will be with thee straight.

PUCK   Follow me, then,
To plainer ground.

Exit Lysander, as following the voice.
Re-enter Demetrius.

DEMETRIUS   Lysander! speak again:

Notes

Notes

> Thou runaway, thou coward, art thou fled? 405
> Speak! In some bush? Where dost thou hide thy head?

PUCK
> Thou coward, art thou bragging to the stars,
> Telling the bushes that thou lookest for wars,
> And wilt not come? Come, recreant; come, thou child;
> I'll whip thee with a rod: he is defiled 410
> That draws a sword on thee.

DEMETRIUS   Yea, art thou there?

PUCK
> Follow my voice: we'll try no manhood here.
>> *Exeunt.*
>> *Re-enter Lysander.*

LYSANDER
> He goes before me and still dares me on:
> When I come where he calls, then he is gone.
> The villain is much lighter-heeled than I: 415
> I followed fast, but faster he did fly;
> That fallen am I in dark uneven way,
> And here will rest me.
>> *[Lies down.]*
> Come, thou gentle day!
> For if but once thou show me thy grey light,
> I'll find Demetrius and revenge this spite. 420
>> *[Sleeps.]*
>> *Re-enter Puck and Demetrius.*

PUCK
> Ho, ho, ho! Coward, why comest thou not?

DEMETRIUS
> Abide me, if thou darest; for well I wot
> Thou runnest before me, shifting every place,
> And darest not stand, nor look me in the face.
> Where art thou now?

PUCK   Come hither: I am here. 425

DEMETRIUS
> Nay, then, thou mockest me. Thou shalt buy this dear,

If ever I thy face by daylight see:
Now, go thy way. Faintness constraineth me
To measure out my length on this cold bed.
By day's approach look to be visited.   430
   [Lies down and sleeps.]
   Re-enter Helena.

HELENA
O weary night, O long and tedious night,
   Abate thy hours! Shine comforts from the east,
That I may back to Athens by daylight,
   From these that my poor company detest:
And sleep, that sometimes shuts up sorrow's eye,   435
Steal me awhile from mine own company.
   [Lies down and sleeps.]

PUCK
   Yet but three? Come one more;
   Two of both kinds makes up four.
   Here she comes, curst and sad:
   Cupid is a knavish lad,   440
   Thus to make poor females mad.
Re-enter Hermia.

HERMIA
Never so weary, never so in woe,
   Bedabbled with the dew and torn with briers,
I can no further crawl, no further go;
   My legs can keep no pace with my desires.   445
Here will I rest me till the break of day.
Heavens shield Lysander, if they mean a fray!
   [Lies down and sleeps.]

PUCK
   On the ground
   Sleep sound:
   I'll apply   450
   To your eye,
   Gentle lover, remedy.
   [Squeezing the juice on Lysander's eyelids.]
      When thou wakest,
      Thou takest

Notes

    True delight   455
     In the sight
   Of thy former lady's eye:
  And the country proverb known,
  That every man should take his own,
  In your waking shall be shown: 460
    Jack shall have Jill;
    Nought shall go ill;
The man shall have his mare again, and all shall be well.
  Exit Puck.

Act IV, Scene 1

Setting: The same.
Lysander, Demetrius, Helena, and Hermia lying asleep.
Enter Titania and Bottom; Peaseblossom, Cobweb, Moth, Mustardseed, and other Fairies attending; Oberon behind, unseen.

TITANIA
    Come, sit thee down upon this flowery bed,
        While I thy amiable cheeks do coy,
    And stick musk-roses in thy sleek smooth head,
        And kiss thy fair large ears, my gentle joy.

BOTTOM: Where's Peaseblossom?

PEASEBLOSSOM: Ready.

BOTTOM: Scratch my head Peaseblossom.
    Where's Mounsieur Cobweb?

COBWEB: Ready.

BOTTOM: Mounsieur Cobweb, good mounsieur, get you
    your weapons in your hand, and kill me a red-hipped
    humble-bee on the top of a thistle; and, good mounsieur,
    bring me the honey-bag. Do not fret yourself too much
    in the action, mounsieur; and, good mounsieur, have a
    care the honey-bag break not; I would be loath to have
    you overflown with a honey-bag, signior. Where's
    Mounsieur Mustardseed?

MUSTARDSEED: Ready.

BOTTOM: Give me your neaf, Mounsieur Mustardseed.
    Pray you, leave your courtesy, good mounsieur.

MUSTARDSEED: What's your will?

BOTTOM: Nothing, good mounsieur, but to help Cavalery
    Peaseblossom to scratch. I must to the barber's, monsieur; for
    methinks I am marvellous hairy about the face; and I
    am such a tender ass, if my hair do but tickle me,
    I must scratch.

TITANIA
    What, wilt thou hear some music, my sweet love?

BOTTOM: I have a reasonable good ear in music. Let's

Notes

"Neaf" means fist. Bottom is asking to shake Mustardseed's hand, rather than receive Mustardseed's continual formal bowing.

have the tongs and the bones.
    Music plays.

TITANIA
Or say, sweet love, what thou desirest to eat. 30

BOTTOM: Truly, a peck of provender: I could munch your good dry oats. Methinks I have a great desire to a bottle of hay: good hay, sweet hay, hath no fellow.

TITANIA
I have a venturous fairy that shall seek
The squirrel's hoard, and fetch thee new nuts. 35

BOTTOM: I had rather have a handful or two of dried peas. But, I pray you, let none of your people stir me: I have an exposition of sleep come upon me.

TITANIA
Sleep thou, and I will wind thee in my arms.
Fairies, begone, and be all ways away. 40
    Exeunt fairies.
So doth the woodbine the sweet honeysuckle
Gently entwist; the female ivy so
Enrings the barky fingers of the elm.
O, how I love thee! how I dote on thee!
    [They sleep.]
    Enter Puck.

OBERON *[Advancing.]*
Welcome, good Robin. Seeest thou this sweet sight? 45
Her dotage now I do begin to pity:
For, meeting her of late behind the wood,
Seeking sweet favours from this hateful fool,
I did upbraid her and fall out with her;
For she his hairy temples then had rounded 50
With a coronet of fresh and fragrant flowers;
And that same dew, which sometime on the buds
Was wont to swell like round and orient pearls,
Stood now within the pretty flowerets' eyes
Like tears that did their own disgrace bewail. 55
When I had at my pleasure taunted her,
And she in mild terms begged my patience,
I then did ask of her her changeling child;

Which straight she gave me, and her fairy sent
To bear him to my bower in fairy land. 60
And now I have the boy, I will undo
This hateful imperfection of her eyes:
And, gentle Puck, take this transformed scalp
From off the head of this Athenian swain;
That, he awaking when the other do, 65
May all to Athens back again repair
And think no more of this night's accidents
But as the fierce vexation of a dream.
But first I will release the fairy queen.
   [Squeezing the herb on her eyelids.]
   Be as thou wast wont to be; 70
   See as thou wast wont to see:
   Dian's bud o'er Cupid's flower
   Hath such force and blessed power.
Now, my Titania; wake you, my sweet queen.

TITANIA
   My Oberon! What visions have I seen! 75
   Methought I was enamoured of an ass.

OBERON
   There lies your love.

TITANIA   How came these things to pass?
   O, how mine eyes do loathe his visage now!

OBERON
   Silence awhile. Robin, take off this head.
   Titania, music call; and strike more dead 80
   Than common sleep of all these five the sense.

TITANIA
   Music, ho! music, such as charmeth sleep!
     Soft music.

PUCK
   [Removes the ass head.]
   Now, when thou wakest, with thine own fool's eyes peep.

OBERON
   Sound, music!
     Louder music.

Notes

Notes

        Come, my queen, take hands with me,
And rock the ground whereon these sleepers be.   85
[Dancing.]
Now thou and I are new in amity,
And will to-morrow midnight solemnly
Dance in Duke Theseus' house triumphantly,
And bless it to all fair prosperity:
There shall the pairs of faithful lovers be   90
Wedded, with Theseus, all in jollity.

PUCK
 Fairy king, attend, and mark:
 I do hear the morning lark.

OBERON
 Then, my queen, in silence sad,
 Trip we after the night's shade: 95
 We the globe can compass soon,
 Swifter than the wandering moon.

TITANIA
 Come, my lord, and in our flight
 Tell me how it came this night
 That I sleeping here was found   100
 With these mortals on the ground.

Exeunt.

Horns winded.

Enter Theseus, Hippolyta, Egeus, and train.

THESEUS
Go, one of you, find out the forester;
For now our observation is performed;
And since we have the vaward of the day,
My love shall hear the music of my hounds.   105
Uncouple in the western valley; let them go:
Dispatch, I say, and find the forester.
 Exit an Attendant.
We will, fair queen, up to the mountain's top,
And mark the musical confusion
Of hounds and echo in conjunction.   110

HIPPOLYTA
 I was with Hercules and Cadmus once,

When in a wood of Crete they bayed the bear
With hounds of Sparta: never did I hear
Such gallant chiding: for, besides the groves,
The skies, the fountains, every region near 115
Seemed all one mutual cry: I never heard
So musical a discord, such sweet thunder.

THESEUS
My hounds are bred out of the Spartan kind,
So flewed, so sanded, and their heads are hung
With ears that sweep away the morning dew; 120
Crook-kneed, and dew-lapped like Thessalian bulls;
Slow in pursuit, but matched in mouth like bells,
Each under each. A cry more tuneable
Was never holloed to, nor cheered with horn,
In Crete, in Sparta, nor in Thessaly: 125
Judge when you hear. But, soft! What nymphs are these?

EGEUS
My lord, this is my daughter here asleep;
And this, Lysander; this Demetrius is;
This Helena, old Nedar's Helena:
I wonder of their being here together. 130

THESEUS
No doubt they rose up early to observe
The rite of May, and hearing our intent,
Came here in grace our solemnity.
But speak, Egeus; is not this the day
That Hermia should give answer of her choice? 135

EGEUS
It is, my lord.

THESEUS
Go, bid the huntsmen wake them with their horns.
Horns and shouting.
Lysander, Demetrius, Helena, and Hermia wake and start up.
Good morrow, friends. Saint Valentine is past:
Begin these wood-birds but to couple now?

LYSANDER
Pardon, my lord.

Notes

Notes

THESEUS   I pray you all, stand up.   140
    I know you two are rival enemies:
    How comes this gentle concord in the world,
    That hatred is so far from jealousy,
    To sleep by hate, and fear no enmity?

LYSANDER
    My lord, I shall reply amazedly,   145
    Half sleep, half waking: but as yet, I swear,
    I cannot truly say how I came here;
    But, as I think,—for truly would I speak,
    And now do I bethink me, so it is,—
    I came with Hermia hither: our intent   150
    Was to be gone from Athens, where we might,
    Without the peril of the Athenian law—

EGEUS
    Enough, enough, my lord; you have enough:
    I beg the law, the law, upon his head.
    They would have stolen away; they would, Demetrius, 155
    Thereby to have defeated you and me—
    You of your wife and me of my consent,
    Of my consent that she should be your wife.

DEMETRIUS
    My lord, fair Helen told me of their stealth,
    Of this their purpose hither to this wood;   160
    And I in fury hither followed them,
    Fair Helena in fancy following me.
    But, my good lord, I wot not by what power,—
    But by some power it is,—my love to Hermia,
    Melted as the snow, seems to me now   165
    As the remembrance of an idle gaud
    Which in my childhood I did dote upon;
    And all the faith, the virtue of my heart,
    The object and the pleasure of mine eye,
    Is only Helena. To her, my lord,   170
    Was I betrothed ere I saw Hermia:
    But, like in sickness, did I loathe this food;
    But, as in health, come to my natural taste,
    Now I do wish it, love it, long for it,
    And will for evermore be true to it.   175

THESEUS
   Fair lovers, you are fortunately met:
   Of this discourse we more will hear anon.
   Egeus, I will overbear your will;
   For in the temple, by and by, with us
   These couples shall eternally be knit: 180
   And, for the morning now is something worn,
   Our purposed hunting shall be set aside.
    Away with us to Athens; three and three,
   We'll hold a feast in great solemnity.
   Come, Hippolyta.   185
      Exeunt Theseus, Hippolyta, Egeus, and train.

DEMETRIUS
   These things seem small and undistinguishable,
   Like far-off mountains turned into clouds.

HERMIA
   Methinks I see these things with parted eye,
   When every thing seems double.

HELENA   So methinks:
   And I have found Demetrius like a jewel,   190
   Mine own, and not mine own.

DEMETRIUS   Are you sure
   That we are awake? It seems to me
   That yet we sleep, we dream. Do not you think
   The duke was here, and bid us follow him?

HERMIA
   Yea; and my father.

HELENA   And Hippolyta.   195

LYSANDER
   And he did bid us follow to the temple.

DEMETRIUS
   Why, then, we are awake: let's follow him
   And by the way let us recount our dreams.
      Exeunt Demetrius, Hermia, Helena, and Lysander.

BOTTOM: *[Awaking.]* When my cue comes, call me, and I
   will answer: my next is, "Most fair Pyramus." Heigh-ho!   200

Notes

Peter Quince! Flute, the bellows-mender! Snout, the tinker! Starveling! God's my life, stolen hence, and left me asleep! I have had a most rare vision. I have had a dream, past the wit of man to say what dream it was: man is but an ass, if he go about to expound this dream. 205
Methought I was—there is no man can tell what. Methought I was,—and methought I had,—but man is but a patched fool, if he will offer to say what methought I had. The eye of man hath not heard, the ear of man hath not seen, man's hand is not able to 210
taste, his tongue to conceive, nor his heart to report what my dream was. I will get Peter Quince to write a ballad of this dream: it shall be called "Bottom's Dream," because it hath no bottom; and I will sing it in the latter end of a play, before the duke: peradventure, 215
to make it the more gracious, I shall sing it at her death.

Exit Bottom.

Act IV, Scene 2

Setting: Athens, Quince's house.
Enter Quince, Flute, Snout, and Starveling.

> QUINCE: Have you sent to Bottom's house? Is he come home yet?
>
> STARVELING: He cannot be heard of. Out of doubt he is transported.
>
> FLUTE: If he come not, then the play is marred: it goes not forward, doth it?
>
> QUINCE: It is not possible: you have not a man in all Athens able to discharge Pyramus but he.
>
> FLUTE: No, he hath simply the best wit of any handicraft man in Athens.
>
> QUINCE: Yea and the best person too; and he is a very paramour for a sweet voice.
>
> FLUTE: You must say "paragon:" a paramour is, God bless us, a thing of naught.
>
> *Enter Snug.*
>
> SNUG: Masters, the duke is coming from the temple, and there is two or three lords and ladies more married: if our sport had gone forward, we had all been made men.
>
> FLUTE: O sweet bully Bottom! Thus hath he lost sixpence a day during his life; he could not have 'scaped sixpence a day: an the duke had not given him sixpence a day for playing Pyramus, I'll be hanged; he would have deserved it: sixpence a day in Pyramus, or nothing.
>
> *Enter Bottom.*
>
> BOTTOM: Where are these lads? Where are these hearts?
>
> QUINCE: Bottom! O most courageous day! O most happy hour!
>
> BOTTOM: Masters, I am to discourse wonders: but ask me not what; for if I tell you, I am no true Athenian.

Notes

The duke had promised to award selected actors six pence a day for the rest of their lives.

Notes

"Ribands" is an old form of "ribbons"; "pumps" are light shoes.

    I will tell you every thing, right as it fell out.   30

QUINCE: Let us hear, sweet Bottom.

BOTTOM: Not a word of me. All that I will tell you is, that the duke hath dined. Get your apparel together, good strings to your beards, new ribbands to your pumps; meet presently at the palace; every man look 35 o'er his part; for the short and the long is, our play is preferred. In any case, let Thisby have clean linen; and let not him that plays the lion pare his nails, for they shall hang out for the lion's claws. And, most dear actors, eat no onions nor garlic, for we are to utter sweet 40 breath; and I do not doubt but to hear them say it is a sweet comedy. No more words: away! go, away!

    Exeunt.

Act V, Scene 1
Setting: Athens, The palace of Theseus.
Enter Theseus, Hippolyta, Philostrate, Lords and Attendants.

HIPPOLYTA
    'Tis strange, my Theseus, that these lovers speak of.

THESEUS
    More strange than true: I never may believe
    These antique fables, nor these fairy toys.
    Lovers and madmen have such seething brains,
    Such shaping fantasies, that apprehend 5
    More than cool reason ever comprehends.
    The lunatic, the lover and the poet
    Are of imagination all compact:
    One sees more devils than vast hell can hold,
    That is, the madman: the lover, all as frantic, 10
    Sees Helen's beauty in a brow of Egypt:
    The poet's eye, in fine frenzy rolling,
    Doth glance from heaven to earth, from earth to heaven;
    And as imagination bodies forth
    The forms of things unknown, the poet's pen 15
    Turns them to shapes and gives to airy nothing
    A local habitation and a name.
    Such tricks hath strong imagination,
    That if it would but apprehend some joy,
    It comprehends some bringer of that joy; 20
    Or in the night, imagining some fear,
    How easy is a bush supposed a bear!

HIPPOLYTA
    But all the story of the night told over,
    And all their minds transfigured so together,
    More witnesseth than fancy's images 25
    And grows to something of great constancy;
    But, howsoever, strange and admirable.

THESEUS
    Here come the lovers, full of joy and mirth.
        Enter Lysander, Demetrius, Hermia, and Helena.
    Joy, gentle friends! joy and fresh days of love
    Accompany your hearts!

Notes

LYSANDER   More than to us   30
    Wait in your royal walks, your board, your bed!

THESEUS
    Come now; what masques, what dances shall we have,
    To wear away this long age of three hours
    Between our after-supper and bed-time?
    Where is our usual manager of mirth?   35
    What revels are in hand? Is there no play,
    To ease the anguish of a torturing hour?
    Call Philostrate.

PHILOSTRATE   Here, mighty Theseus.

THESEUS
    Say, what abridgement have you for this evening?
    What masque? what music? How shall we beguile   40
    The lazy time, if not with some delight?

PHILOSTRATE
    There is a brief how many sports are ripe:
    Make choice of which your highness will see first.
        [Giving a paper.]

THESEUS *[Reads]*
    "The battle with the Centaurs, to be sung
    By an Athenian eunuch to the harp."   45
    We'll none of that: that have I told my love,
    In glory of my kinsman Hercules.
    [Reads] "The riot of the tipsy Bacchanals,
    Tearing the Thracian singer in their rage."
    That is an old device; and it was played   50
    When I from Thebes came last a conqueror.
    [Reads] "The thrice three Muses mourning for the death
    Of Learning, late deceased in beggary."
    That is some satire, keen and critical,
    Not sorting with a nuptial ceremony.   55
    [Reads] "A tedious brief scene of young Pyramus
    And his love Thisby; very tragical mirth."
    Merry and tragical! tedious and brief!
    That is, hot ice and wondrous strange snow.
    How shall we find the concord of this discord?   60

PHILOSTRATE
    A play there is, my lord, some ten words long,
    Which is as brief as I have known a play;
    But by ten words, my lord, it is too long,
    Which makes it tedious; for in all the play
    There is not one word apt, one player fitted: 65
    And tragical, my noble lord, it is;
    For Pyramus therein doth kill himself.
    Which, when I saw rehearsed, I must confess,
    Made mine eyes water; but more merry tears
    The passion of loud laughter never shed.   70

THESEUS
    What are they that do play it?

PHILOSTRATE
    Hard-handed men that work in Athens here,
    Which never laboured in their minds till now,
    And now have toiled their unbreathed memories
    With this same play, against your nuptial.   75

THESEUS
    And we will hear it.

PHILOSTRATE   No, my noble lord;
    It is not for you: I have heard it over,
    And it is nothing, nothing in the world;
    Unless you can find sport in their intents,
    Extremely stretched and conned with cruel pain,   80
    To do you service.

THESEUS   I will hear that play;
    For never anything can be amiss,
    When simpleness and duty tender it.
    Go, bring them in: and take your places, ladies.
    Exit Philostrate.

HIPPOLYTA
    I love not to see wretchedness o'er charged   85
    And duty in his service perishing.

THESEUS
    Why, gentle sweet, you shall see no such thing.

Notes

HIPPOLYTA
   He says they can do nothing in this kind.

THESEUS
   The kinder we, to give them thanks for nothing.
   Our sport shall be to take what they mistake: 90
   And what poor duty cannot do, noble respect
   Takes it in might, not merit.
   Where I have come, great clerks have purposed
   To greet me with premeditated welcomes;
   Where I have seen them shiver and look pale,   95
   Make periods in the midst of sentences,
   Throttle their practised accent in their fears
   And in conclusion dumbly have broke off,
   Not paying me a welcome. Trust me, sweet,
   Out of this silence yet I picked a welcome;   100
   And in the modesty of fearful duty
   I read as much as from the rattling tongue
   Of saucy and audacious eloquence.
   Love, therefore, and tongue-tied simplicity
   In least speak most, to my capacity.   105

     Re-enter Philostrate.

PHILOSTRATE
   So please your grace, the Prologue is addressed.

THESEUS
   Let him approach.

     Flourish of trumpets.
     Enter Quince for the Prologue.

QUINCE
   If we offend, it is with our good will.
     That you should think, we come not to offend,
   But with good will. To show our simple skill,   110
     That is the true beginning of our end.
   Consider then we come but in despite.
     We do not come as minding to contest you,
   Our true intent is. All for your delight
     We are not here. That you should here repent you,   115
   The actors are at hand and by their show
   You shall know all that you are like to know.

THESEUS: This fellow doth not stand upon points.

LYSANDER: He hath rid his prologue like a rough colt; he
knows not the stop. A good moral, my lord: it is not   120
enough to speak, but to speak true.

HIPPOLYTA: Indeed he hath played on this prologue like a
child on a recorder; a sound, but not in government.

THESEUS: His speech was like a tangled chain; nothing
impaired, but all disordered. Who is next?   125

Enter Pyramus and Thisby, Wall, Moonshine, and Lion.

QUINCE
   Gentles, perchance you wonder at this show;
      But wonder on, till truth make all things plain.
   This man is Pyramus, if you would know;
      This beauteous lady Thisby is certain.
   This man, with lime and rough-cast, doth present   130
      Wall, that vile Wall which did these lovers sunder;
   And through Wall's chink, poor souls, they are content
      To whisper. At the which let no man wonder.
   This man, with lanthorn, dog, and bush of thorn,
      Presenteth Moonshine; for, if you will know,   135
   By moonshine did these lovers think no scorn
      To meet at Ninus' tomb, there, there to woo.
   This grisly beast, which Lion hight by name,
   The trusty Thisby, coming first by night,
   Did scare away, or rather did affright;   140
   And, as she fled, her mantle she did fall,
      Which Lion vile with bloody mouth did stain.
   Anon comes Pyramus, sweet youth and tall,
      And finds his trusty Thisby's mantle slain:
   Whereat, with blade, with bloody blameful blade,   145
      He bravely broached his boiling bloody breast;
   And Thisby, tarrying in mulberry shade,
      His dagger drew, and died. For all the rest,
   Let Lion, Moonshine, Wall, and lovers twain
   At large discourse, while here they do remain.   150

Exeunt Quince, Pyramus, Thisby, Lion, and Moonshine.

THESEUS: I wonder if the lion be to speak.

Notes

DEMETRIUS: No wonder, my lord: one lion may, when many asses do.

SNOUT
In this same interlude it doth befall
That I, one Snout by name, present a wall; 155
And such a wall, as I would have you think,
That had in it a crannied hole or chink,
Through which the lovers, Pyramus and Thisby,
Did whisper often very secretly.
This loam, this rough-cast and this stone doth show 160
That I am that same wall; the truth is so:
And this the cranny is, right and sinister,
Through which the fearful lovers are to whisper.

THESEUS: Would you desire lime and hair to speak better? 165

DEMETRIUS: It is the wittiest partition that ever I heard discourse, my lord.

Enter Pyramus.

THESEUS: Pyramus draws near the wall: silence!

BOTTOM [As Pyramus]
O grim-looked night! O night with hue so black!
O night, which ever art when day is not! 170
O night, O night! alack, alack, alack,
I fear my Thisby's promise is forgot!
And thou, O wall, O sweet, O lovely wall,
That standest between her father's ground and mine!
Thou wall, O wall, O sweet and lovely wall, 175
Show me thy chink, to blink through with mine eyne!
[Wall holds up his fingers.]
Thanks, courteous wall: Jove shield thee well for this!
But what see I? No Thisby do I see.
O wicked wall, through whom I see no bliss!
Cursed be thy stones for thus deceiving me! 180

THESEUS: The wall, methinks, being sensible, should curse again.

BOTTOM: No, in truth, sir, he should not. "Deceiving me" is Thisby's cue: she is to enter now, and I am to

spy her through the wall. You shall see, it will 185
fall pat as I told you. Yonder she comes.
 Enter Thisby.

FLUTE *[As Thisby]*
 O wall, full often hast thou heard my moans,
  For parting my fair Pyramus and me!
 My cherry lips have often kissed thy stones,
  Thy stones with lime and hair knit up in thee. 190

BOTTOM *[As Pyramus]*
 I see a voice: now will I to the chink,
 To spy an I can hear my Thisby's face. Thisby!

FLUTE *[As Thisby]*
 My love thou art, my love, I think.

BOTTOM *[As Pyramus]*
 Think what thou wilt, I am thy lover's grace;
 And, like Limander, am I trusty still. 195

FLUTE *[As Thisby]*
 And I like Helen, till the Fates me kill.

BOTTOM *[As Pyramus]*
 Not Shafalus to Procrus was so true.

FLUTE *[As Thisby]*
 As Shafalus to Procrus, I to you.

BOTTOM *[As Pyramus]*
 O kiss me through the hole of this vile wall!

FLUTE *[As Thisby]*
 I kiss the wall's hole, not your lips at all. 200

BOTTOM *[As Pyramus]*
 Wilt thou at Ninny's tomb meet me straightway?

FLUTE *[As Thisby]*
 'Tide life, 'tide death, I come without delay.
 Exeunt Pyramus and Thisby.

SNOUT *[As Wall]*
 Thus have I, Wall, my part discharged so;
 And, being done, thus Wall away doth go.
 Exit Snout.

Notes

This section is full of mixed-up names and stories' characters.

Notes

THESEUS: Now is the mural down between the two neighbours. 205

DEMETRIUS: No remedy, my lord, when walls are so wilful to hear without warning.

HIPPOLYTA: This is the silliest stuff that ever I heard.

THESEUS: The best in this kind are but shadows; and the worst are no worse, if imagination amend them. 210

HIPPOLYTA: It must be your imagination then, and not theirs.

THESEUS: If we imagine no worse of them than they of themselves, they may pass for excellent men. Here come two noble beasts in, a man and a lion. 215

Enter Lion and Moonshine.

SNUG
   You, ladies, you, whose gentle hearts do fear
      The smallest monstrous mouse that creeps on floor,
   May now perchance both quake and tremble here,
      When lion rough in wildest rage doth roar. 220
   Then know that I, as Snug the joiner, am
   A lion-fell, nor else no lion's dam;
   For, if I should as lion come in strife
   Into this place, 'twere pity on my life.

THESEUS: A very gentle beast, and of a good conscience. 225

DEMETRIUS: The very best at a beast, my lord, that e'er I saw.

LYSANDER: This lion is a very fox for his valour.

THESEUS: True; and a goose for his discretion.

DEMETRIUS: Not so, my lord; for his valour cannot carry his discretion; and the fox carries the goose. 230

THESEUS: His discretion, I am sure, cannot carry his valour; for the goose carries not the fox. It is well: leave it to his discretion, and let us listen to the moon.

STARVELING [*As Moonshine*]
   This lanthorn doth the horned moon present;— 235

DEMETRIUS: He should have worn the horns on his head.

THESEUS: He is no crescent, and his horns are invisible within the circumference.

STARVELING [As Moonshine]
This lanthorn doth the horned moon present;
Myself the man i' the moon do seem to be.   240

THESEUS: This is the greatest error of all the rest: the man should be put into the lanthorn. How is it else the man i' the moon?

DEMETRIUS: He dares not come there for the candle; for, you see, it is already in snuff.   245

HIPPOLYTA: I am aweary of this moon: would he would change!

THESEUS: It appears, by his small light of discretion, that he is in the wane; but yet, in courtesy, in all reason, we must stay the time.   250

LYSANDER: Proceed, Moon.

STARVELING: All that I have to say, is, to tell you that the lanthorn is the moon; I, the man i' the moon; this thorn-bush, my thorn-bush; and this dog, my dog.

DEMETRIUS: Why, all these should be in the lanthorn;   255
for all these are in the moon. But, silence! here comes Thisby.

Enter Thisby.

FLUTE [As Thisby]
This is old Ninny's tomb. Where is my love?

SNUG [As Lion] [Roaring] O!
Thisby runs off.

DEMETRIUS: Well roared, Lion.   260

THESEUS: Well run, Thisby.

HIPPOLYTA: Well shone, Moon. Truly, the moon shines with a good grace.

The Lion shakes Thisby's dropped mantle and exits.

Notes

THESEUS: Well moused, Lion.

DEMETRIUS: And then came Pyramus. 265

LYSANDER: And so the lion vanished.

Enter Pyramus.

BOTTOM *[As Pyramus]*
    Sweet Moon, I thank thee for thy sunny beams;
        I thank thee, Moon, for shining now so bright;
    For, by thy gracious, golden, glittering gleams,
        I trust to take of truest Thisby sight. 270
            But stay, O spite!
            But mark, poor knight,
        What dreadful dole is here!
            Eyes, do you see?
            How can it be? 275
        O dainty duck! O dear!
            Thy mantle good,
        What, stained with blood!
        Approach, ye Furies fell!
            O Fates, come, come, 280
        Cut thread and thrum;
        Quail, crush, conclude, and quell!

THESEUS: This passion, and the death of a dear friend,
    would go near to make a man look sad.

HIPPOLYTA: Beshrew my heart, but I pity the man. 285

BOTTOM *[As Pyramus]*
    O wherefore, Nature, didst thou lions frame?
        Since lion vile hath here deflowered my dear:
    Which is—no, no—which was the fairest dame
        That lived, that loved, that liked, that looked with cheer.
            Come, tears, confound; 290
            Out, sword, and wound
        The pap of Pyramus;
            Ay, that left pap,
        Where heart doth hop: *[Stabs himself.]*
    Thus die I, thus, thus, thus. 295
        Now am I dead,
        Now am I fled;
    My soul is in the sky:

        Tongue, lose thy light;
        Moon take thy flight: 300
    Exit Moonshine.
        Now die, die, die, die, die.
    [*Pyramus dies.*]

DEMETRIUS: No die, but an ace, for him; for he is but one.

LYSANDER: Less than an ace, man; for he is dead; he is nothing.

THESEUS: With the help of a surgeon he might yet   305
recover, and prove an ass.

HIPPOLYTA: How chance Moonshine is gone before Thisby comes back and finds her lover?

    Re-enter Thisby.

THESEUS: She will find him by starlight. Here she comes; and her passion ends the play.   310

HIPPOLYTA: Methinks she should not use a long one for such a Pyramus: I hope she will be brief.

DEMETRIUS: A mote will turn the balance, which Pyramus, which Thisby, is the better; he for a man, God warrant us; she for a woman, God bless us.   315

LYSANDER: She hath spied him already with those sweet eyes.

DEMETRIUS: And thus she means, videlicet:—

FLUTE [*As Thisby*]
    Asleep, my love?
    What, dead, my dove?   320
  O Pyramus, arise!
    Speak, speak. Quite dumb?
    Dead, dead? A tomb
  Must cover thy sweet eyes.
    These lily lips,   325
    This cherry nose,
  These yellow cowslip cheeks,
      Are gone, are gone:
      Lovers, make moan:
  His eyes were green as leeks.   330

Notes

Videlicet *means* "*as you see.*"

Notes

    O Sisters Three,
      Come, come to me,
  With hands as pale as milk;
      Lay them in gore,
      Since you have shore   335
  With shears his thread of silk.
      Tongue, not a word:
      Come, trusty sword;
  Come, blade, my breast imbrue: *[Stabs herself.]*
      And, farewell, friends;   340
      Thus Thisby ends:
      Adieu, adieu, adieu.
[Thisby dies.]
Enter Lion, Moonshine, and Wall.

THESEUS: Moonshine and Lion are left to bury the dead.

DEMETRIUS: Ay, and Wall too.

BOTTOM: *[Starting up]*
  No, I assure you; the wall is down that parted their   345
  fathers. Will it please you to see the epilogue, or to hear
  a Bergomask dance between two of our company?

THESEUS. No epilogue, I pray you; for your play needs
  no excuse. Never excuse; for when the players are all
  dead, there need none to be blamed. Marry, if he   350
  that writ it had played Pyramus and hanged himself
  in Thisby's garter, it would have been a fine tragedy: and
  so it is, truly; and very notably discharged. But come,
  your Bergomask: let your epilogue alone.
    [A dance.]
The iron tongue of midnight hath told twelve: 355
Lovers, to bed; 'tis almost fairy time.
I fear we shall out-sleep the coming morn
As much as we this night have overwatched.
This palpable-gross play hath well beguiled
The heavy gait of night. Sweet friends, to bed.   360
A fortnight hold we this solemnity,
In nightly revels and new jollity.
  Exeunt.
  Enter Puck.

PUCK

    Now the hungry lion roars,
        And the wolf behowls the moon;
    Whilst the heavy ploughman snores,   365
        All with weary task fordone.
    Now the wasted brands do glow,
        Whilst the screech-owl, screeching loud,
    Puts the wretch that lies in woe
        In remembrance of a shroud.   370
    Now it is the time of night
        That the graves all gaping wide,
    Every one lets forth his sprite,
        In the church-way paths to glide:
    And we fairies, that do run   375
        By the triple Hecate's team
    From the presence of the sun,
        Following darkness like a dream,
    Now are frolic: not a mouse
    Shall disturb this hallowed house: 380
    I am sent with broom before,
    To sweep the dust behind the door.

Enter Oberon and Titania with their train.

OBERON

    Through the house give glimmering light,
        By the dead and drowsy fire:
    Every elf and fairy sprite   385
        Hop as light as bird from brier;
    And this ditty, after me,
    Sing, and dance it trippingly.

TITANIA

    First, rehearse your song by rote
    To each word a warbling note: 390
    Hand in hand, with fairy grace,
    Will we sing, and bless this place.

[Song and dance.]

OBERON

    Now, until the break of day,
    Through this house each fairy stray.
    To the best bride-bed will we,   395

Notes

Notes

    Which by us shall blessed be;
    And the issue there create
    Ever shall be fortunate.
    So shall all the couples three
    Ever true in loving be;   400
    And the blots of Nature's hand
    Shall not in their issue stand;
    Never mole, hare lip, nor scar,
    Nor mark prodigious, such as are
    Despised in nativity,   405
    Shall upon their children be.
    With this field-dew consecrate,
    Every fairy take his gait;
    And each several chamber bless,
    Through this palace, with sweet peace;   410
    And the owner of it blest
    Ever shall in safety rest.
    Trip away; make no stay;
    Meet me all by break of day.

Exeunt Oberon, Titania, and train.

PUCK

    If we shadows have offended,   415
    Think but this, and all is mended,
    That you have but slumbered here
    While these visions did appear.
    And this weak and idle theme,
    No more yielding but a dream,   420
    Gentles, do not reprehend:
    If you pardon, we will mend:
    And, as I am an honest Puck,
    If we have unearned luck
    Now to 'scape the serpent's tongue,   425
    We will make amends ere long;
    Else the Puck a liar call;
    So, good night unto you all.
    Give me your hands, if we be friends,
    And Robin shall restore amends.   430

Exit Puck.